D1202785

Feel free to enjoy
my mom and aunt's
book — Both awesome
women

When done
passing this book
(sharing)
Call me + I'll
pick it up
Sincerly Sharon
Rochelle Balsberg
416-532-2304

THE AZRIELI SERIES OF HOLOCAUST SURVIVOR MEMOIRS:
PUBLISHED TITLES

ENGLISH TITLES

Never Far Apart

Kitty Salsberg and Ellen Foster

THE AZRIELI FOUNDATION
www.azrielifoundation.org

Cover and book design by Mark Goldstein
Endpaper maps by Martin Gilbert
Map on page xxxi by François Blanc

LIBRARY AND ARCHIVES CANADA CATALOGUING IN PUBLICATION

Salsberg, Kitty, 1932–, author
    Never far apart / Kitty Salsberg and Ellen Foster.

(Azrieli series of Holocaust survivor memoirs. Series 7)
Includes index.
ISBN 978-1-897470-87-9 (paperback)

1. Salsberg, Kitty, 1932–. 2. Foster, Ellen, 1935–. 3. Holocaust, Jewish (1939–1945) – Hungary – Personal narratives. 4. Holocaust survivors – Canada – Biography. I. Foster, Ellen, 1935–, author II. Azrieli Foundation, issuing body III. Title. IV. Series: Azrieli series of Holocaust survivor memoirs; Series 7

DS135.H93S26 2015   940.53'18092   C2015-906063-X

PRINTED IN CANADA

The Azrieli Series of Holocaust Survivor Memoirs

Naomi Azrieli, Publisher

Jody Spiegel, Program Director
Arielle Berger, Managing Editor
Elizabeth Lasserre, Senior Editor, French-Language Editions
Farla Klaiman, Editor
Elin Beaumont, Senior Educational Outreach and Events Coordinator
Catherine Person, Educational Outreach and Events Coordinator,
    Quebec and French Canada
Marc-Olivier Cloutier, Educational Outreach and Events Assistant,
    Quebec and French Canada
Tim MacKay, Digital Platform Manager
Elizabeth Banks, Digital Asset and Archive Curator
Susan Roitman, Office Manager (Toronto)
Mary Mellas, Executive Assistant and Human Resources (Montreal)

Mark Goldstein, Art Director
François Blanc, Cartographer
Bruno Paradis, Layout, French-language editions

Contents

Series Preface:
In their own words. . .

In telling these stories, the writers have liberated themselves. For so many years we did not speak about it, even when we became free people living in a free society. Now, when at last we are writing about what happened to us in this dark period of history, knowing that our stories will be read and live on, it is possible for us to feel truly free. These unique historical documents put a face on what was lost, and allow readers to grasp the enormity of what happened to six million Jews – one story at a time.

David J. Azrieli, C.M., C.Q., M.Arch
Holocaust survivor and founder, The Azrieli Foundation

Since the end of World War II, over 30,000 Jewish Holocaust survivors have immigrated to Canada. Who they are, where they came from, what they experienced and how they built new lives for themselves and their families are important parts of our Canadian heritage. The Azrieli Foundation's Holocaust Survivor Memoirs Program was established to preserve and share the memoirs written by those who survived the twentieth-century Nazi genocide of the Jews of Europe and later made their way to Canada. The program is guided by the conviction that each survivor of the Holocaust has a remarkable story to tell, and that such stories play an important role in education about tolerance and diversity.

Millions of individual stories are lost to us forever. By preserving the stories written by survivors and making them widely available to a broad audience, the Azrieli Foundation's Holocaust Survivor Memoirs Program seeks to sustain the memory of all those who perished at the hands of hatred, abetted by indifference and apathy. The personal accounts of those who survived against all odds are as different as the people who wrote them, but all demonstrate the courage, strength, wit and luck that it took to prevail and survive in such terrible adversity. The memoirs are also moving tributes to people – strangers and friends – who risked their lives to help others, and who, through acts of kindness and decency in the darkest of moments, frequently helped the persecuted maintain faith in humanity and courage to endure. These accounts offer inspiration to all, as does the survivors' desire to share their experiences so that new generations can learn from them.

The Holocaust Survivor Memoirs Program collects, archives and publishes these distinctive records and the print editions are available free of charge to educational institutions and Holocaust-education programs across Canada. They are also available for sale to the general public at bookstores. All revenues to the Azrieli Foundation from the sales of the Azrieli Series of Holocaust Survivor Memoirs go toward the publishing and educational work of the memoirs program.

The Azrieli Foundation would like to express appreciation to the following people for their invaluable efforts in producing this book: Doris Bergen, Sherry Dodson (Maracle Press), Joan Eadie, Allegra Robinson, Beverly Solotov, and Margie Wolfe and Emma Rodgers of Second Story Press.

About the Glossary

The following memoir contains a number of terms, concepts and historical references that may be unfamiliar to the reader. For information on major organizations; significant historical events and people; geographical locations; religious and cultural terms; and foreign-language words and expressions that will help give context and background to the events described in the text, please see the glossary beginning on page 135.

Introduction

"I am like the Joshua Tree that grows in the Mojave Desert. It stands firmly in the ground, through hot days and cold nights, surviving the harsh dryness with hardly a drop of water and withstanding the cruel winds that batter it. No matter what, it lives on, grounded."

Stretched across California's Colorado and Mojave deserts, the Joshua Tree National Park is home to hundreds of diverse plant and animal species. At nearly 800,000 acres or some 3,300 square kilometres, the hostile expanse is defined by unforgiving landscapes and an unpredictable climate. The park's namesake Joshua trees are a significant feature of the Mojave Desert's ecosystem.

Like the tree, Ilonka Mozes-Nagy perceived her life as starting in a desert, and her formative years as having taken place in an unforgiving climate. Both she and her older sister, Kati, were raised under volatile conditions in Budapest; though shaken and scarred by Nazism, they withstood both the wartime traumas and the challenges of life in post-war Canada. Like the Joshua tree, their roots remained firmly planted.

Never Far Apart is a poetic and reflexive remembrance of two sisters who survived the Holocaust. Honest and unapologetic, the sisters' eyewitness accounts seamlessly intertwine as a cohesive collection of memories. The volume is distinctive among survivor memoirs stylistically and in terms of the nuanced portrait it paints of Jewish Budapest, life under Nazism and the struggles of post-war rehabilitation. The two narratives – recorded separately and thousands of miles apart by Kati and Ilonka Mozes-Nagy, now known by the Anglicized names Kitty Salsberg and Ellen Foster – complement each other with juxtaposing views on a series of shared experiences. Speaking to the complexity of families and their dynamics, the memoir explores how relationships – between husband and wife, parent and child, and between siblings – were affected by the Holocaust, and how family and the notion of home shifted in the shadow of liberation.

By a circumstance of fate, I was born a Jew in Canada of the 1980s, and raised in a society that celebrated democracy, multiculturalism, rights and freedoms for all of its citizens. A bookish youth, my personal first encounters with the Holocaust came early and in the form of heroic protagonists in young adult novels. These accounts of Jewish youth, courageous beyond their years, had a transformative effect. Yet I had difficulty comprehending such stories; Nazi Germany seemed like an alternate universe light years away from my comfortable Toronto upbringing. It was a planet populated by insane dictators, sadistic militants and brainwashed followers. How could members of the human race – my human race – believe such hateful ideology? Even less explained, how could anyone, let alone a child, survive these expressions of hate?

The history that I later discovered proved far more shocking. As my intellectual curiosity developed, the mythologized National Socialism and "war on the Jews" that once leapt off the pages of skillfully written novels grew clearer. I became aware that Holocaust survivors existed within my own community. Stories I once consumed through a fictional lens entered my lexicon in another form: the survivor memoir. These memoirs contributed to my overall knowledge of the events of the Holocaust. Unlike other sources, often dry and detached, and shared through the lens of the perpetrator, memoirs provide complex and individual perspectives on trauma, survival and ethical decision-making in moments of crisis. Told from the perspective of two child survivors, war orphans to Canada, *Never Far Apart* is no exception.

~

While Kati and Ilonka were not born until the 1930s, international events triggered by the World War I era set the stage for the difficulties they would soon face. The aftermath of the war signalled a sea of change on the European stage. Mass upheaval, a refugee crisis and harsh treaties imposed on the defeated by the triumphant Allied powers culminated in the re-making of national borders. The Treaty of Versailles (June 28, 1919) left a devastating and significant mark on Germany; impossible reparation payment demands, the forced acceptance of the war guilt clause, the dismantling of the army and territorial losses led to volatile conditions. Popular support for nationalist right-wing politics and ideologies subsequently increased, culminating in the 1933 election of Adolf Hitler's National Socialist German Workers' Party (NSDAP or Nazi Party). The consequences of this ascension eventually had global ramifications.

Being on the losing side of World War I caused the collapse of the Austro-Hungarian Empire. The conditions of the Treaty of Trianon (June 1920) prompted the establishment of an independent and ethnically diverse Hungary with substantially reduced physical size, as it ceded 60 per cent of its pre-war territory to the newly-formed Czechoslovakia. Taking advantage of the country's instabilities, Hungarian fascist leader Ferenc Szálasi merged four fascist groups to establish the Party of National Will (1935), later renamed the Arrow Cross Party (1939). Rooted in pan-nationalism, anti-Communism and antisemitism, the Arrow Cross assumed the position of official opposition in parliament in the late 1930s, compromising the existence of the Mozes-Nagy family and all of Hungarian Jewry.

During the interwar period, Budapest's Jews experienced two decades of assimilation, coupled by high rates of intermarriage and conversion among upwardly mobile urban dwellers, in the new Hungary. Jews continued to face latent antisemitism and quota systems that limited participation in various industries and higher education. Despite these restrictions, Jews made significant contributions to the political, cultural and economic fabric of Hungarian society. The landscape also boasted a rich and diverse Jewish culture, featuring a wealth of religious educational institutions, Zionist youth movements and sports associations. Some 825,000 Jews (representing less than 10 per cent of the country's total population, including newly annexed territories) resided in Hungary when it entered World War II with the Axis alliance; 200,000 Jews, including Kati and Ilonka's family, called Budapest home.

The Mozes-Nagy sisters' earliest memories formed against the backdrop of poverty, exclusion and upheaval, in both their home and their country. Due to economic stressors, their parents' marital discord and bouts of illness – dysentery for Ilonka, tuberculosis for Kati – the girls spent much of their childhoods apart. While Ilonka remained with her mother, Borishka, Kati found solace in her maternal grandparents' comfortable apartment. These extended separations without parental explanation influenced the memories that accompanied each sister on their adventures.

Kati's earliest adventure involved crossing a village road, gripping Ilonka's hand and attempting to avoid a flock of territorial geese. Escaping danger became a recurring theme in the girls' lives, as did their ability to survive assault. Other recollections were bittersweet: a one-bedroom apartment without hot water, electricity or an indoor bathroom; singing and dancing on tabletops at the nightclub where her father, the charming Romanian-born Marton, worked as a salesman; and eating sweets late at night after his return home. Less pleasant experiences of pre-war life, including her mother's depression and the family's financial struggles, were repressed, with the details later filled in by Ilonka.

As the sisters navigated their complex home life, the situation for

Jews in Hungary became increasingly unstable. A popular misconception is that Hungary's Jews remained impervious to deportation before the German invasion of March 1944. While they were the final Jewish population to succumb to Nazism, organized attacks on Magyar Jews by Hungarian fascists dated back to the late 1930s and the strengthening of German-Hungarian relations. Hoping to win favour, Germany orchestrated Hungary's reclaiming of Magyar-stronghold territories in Slovakia and Carpatho-Ukraine, areas that had been ceded to Czechoslovakia (Vienna Awards, 1938/1940).

In October 1940, Hungary officially joined the Axis alliance.[1] The years leading up to this alliance signalled the arrival of the second cloud to loom over Kati and Ilonka's lives. Between 1938 and 1941, a series of decrees focused on eliminating internal "threats" to national values were introduced in the Hungarian parliament. The first decree enacted on May 28, 1938, defined Jews by religious affiliation, and formally sealed the community's disenfranchisement by limiting Jewish participation to 20 per cent in civil service, industries and institutes of higher learning. The following May, the noose tightened further on Jewish representation in industry and business, pushing many Jews into poverty. This time, however, the delineation of "Jewish" expanded to align with Germany's infamous Nuremberg Laws. Now, members of the "Israelite faith," or any person with two Jewish grandparents – including 100,000 Hungarian converts to Christianity and their offspring – fell victim to these laws. A third decree criminalized marriages between Jews and non-Jews.

The second decree contained a devastating blow to the country's Jews. In an effort to eliminate allegedly untrustworthy elements from

---

1 For comprehensive English-language sketches of the Holocaust in Hungary, see Randolph L. Braham, *The Nazis' Last Victims: The Holocaust in Hungary* (Detroit: Wayne State University Press, 2002); and László Csősz, Gábor Kádár and Zoltán Vági, *The Holocaust in Hungary: Evolution of a Genocide,* Documenting Life and Destruction: Holocaust Sources in Context (Lanham, MD: AltaMira Press, 2013).

its ranks, Hungary introduced legislation that stripped Jews of the right to bear arms and ordered the conscription of some 100,000 Jewish men into forced labour battalions. Despite second-class categorization and latent antisemitism from non-Jewish units, the labour performed by these battalions was not inherently dangerous during the first two years of service. When Hungary entered the war on the Eastern front in 1942 and Jewish battalions joined the Second Hungarian Army, conditions radically worsened. Deprived of protective gear and food, and publicly identified as Jews, the men were compelled to perform the most dangerous tasks on the battlefront and also faced violent attacks by non-Jewish compatriots. More than half of the men in these battalions lost their lives during the war, among them Marton Mozes-Nagy.

Judaism was of no significance in the girls' lives. Although they did not attend church or celebrate Christmas, as did many of Kati's classmates, their family also did not observe the Sabbath, frequent synagogue or uphold the laws of *kashrut*. Nevertheless, the Nazi-inspired anti-Jewish laws had a deeply painful effect: children chased them with sticks, yelling "dirty Jews" in the streets, while classmates visibly ignored the girls, creating a lonely and anxiety-riddled environment non-conducive to learning. A formerly friendly neighbour's cruel and unrelenting torment drove Ilonka to tears. Kati also experienced a rude awakening about her religious heritage. From everything they heard and experienced, Jewishness meant something negative: "Everyone thought the Jews were very bad people and should not get away with terrible things they supposedly did." Adults offered no explanations for the maltreatment, an experience shared by Jewish children throughout wartime Europe.

~

Hungary's conservative Prime Minister Miklós Kállay and Regent Miklós Horthy resisted pressure to deport the country's Jews until it was clear that Germany would likely lose the war. Having caught on to Kállay's plan to withdraw Hungary from the conflict and switch alliances, Germany invaded its former ally on March 19, 1944. Horthy was allowed to remain Regent of Hungary, but Kállay was ousted from his post and replaced by pro-Nazi General Döme Sztójay, a former Hungarian minister to Berlin. The new prime minister agreed to Hungary's continued participation in the war and to cooperate in the deportations of Hungary's Jews to concentration camps in the east.

The new pro-Nazi government swiftly imposed a Jewish Council in Budapest and introduced debilitating restrictions on the Jewish community.[2] The humiliating yellow *Judenstern* (Star of David badge) was introduced and sewn onto the Mozes-Nagy sisters' outerwear; freedom of movement denied; property and valuables confiscated; and hundreds of Jews sent to the nearby Kistarcsa transit camp. Kati, Ilonka and their remaining relatives were expelled from their apartments and relocated to some of two thousand "Yellow Star" buildings. Any hopes that the community might escape the fate of Jews across occupied Europe were dashed as Hungarian authorities ordered Jews from the outlying provinces to congregate in makeshift ghettos in larger city centres in April 1944.

From May to July of 1944, under the command of Colonel Adolf Eichmann, the SS and Hungarian collaborators deported nearly 440,000 Hungarian Jews. The vast majority went to Auschwitz-Birkenau concentration and death camp, while the remainder became slave labourers building trenches along the Austrian border. By the time the Horthy government halted deportations on July 7, only Budapest's Jews remained.

Frustrated with the Hungarian government's refusal to cooperate with deportations, Germany overthrew the government and put the fascist Arrow Cross Party in power in October 1944. Budapest

---

2 On the establishment of the Budapest Ghetto, refer Tim Cole, *Holocaust City: The Making of a Jewish Ghetto* (London: Routledge, 2003).

Jews saw their reprieve abruptly ended. Within a few short weeks, Arrow Cross guards orchestrated a reign of terror. They summarily shot hundreds of Jews, and drafted many more for slave labour. That November, Arrow Cross officials ordered Budapest's Jews into a closed ghetto, divided between the "international ghetto" for those with protective papers issued by a neutral power, and those without any legal protection. At the same time, more than 70,000 Jews were rounded up and forced on death marches. Thousands died en route to Austria of starvation, exposure and executions. Those who survived the march found themselves in various concentration camps in Austria and Germany.

Through an intervention by an uncle, Kati and Ilonka were deposited at a Red Cross building, a safe house, thus avoiding the fate that befell most of their loved ones. Despite the chaos and violence surrounding them, Kati recalled that she did not feel fear: "I don't know why I did not feel panicky. I suppose that at the age of eleven, one cannot imagine the true meaning of such atrocities." Her sole goal: to keep herself, and Ilonka, alive.

> *The sirens are screaming, the bombs are coming down.*
> *Since our heads are shaved, and we look gaunt and starved,*
> *I want to just lie down and leave this world behind.*
> *My sister found some scraps; she feeds them to me*
> *"Don't give up, Ilonka. You mean the world to me."*
> *She is so protective, trying to do her best*
> *To keep my spirit going, says this war can't last.*
> *Still I want to be babied and loved, like I used to be before*
> *But that's only a pipe dream, since our parents were killed in the war.*

> Ellen Foster, "In the Ghetto of Budapest"

During the siege of Budapest (December 24, 1944 – February 13, 1945), the Arrow Cross rounded up some 20,000 Jews from the

Budapest ghetto and murdered them along the banks of the Danube. Those who escaped the executions lived under the constant threat of bombings, seeking shelter wherever possible in underground cellars, emerging only to forage for food at great personal risk. Kati and Ilonka were among 100,000 Jews remaining in the Budapest ghetto when it was liberated by the Soviet army on January 18, 1945, after close to a month of intense fighting. Having barely staved off starvation thanks to Kati's pluck and resourcefulness, the sisters quickly reunited with their maternal grandparents and members of their mother's extended family. Their mother, Borishka, did not return. It would be years before the girls learned of the circumstances surrounding her death.

After a brief convalescence on a countryside farm, the girls entered a Zionist-run children's home in Budapest, where they began to emotionally recuperate from their wartime traumas, cultivating meaningful friendships and discovering a newfound pride in Judaism. These months stood out as a bright light in an otherwise bleak setting. Borishka's younger sister, Margaret, eventually assumed legal guardianship of the girls.

While Ilonka enjoyed her post-war return to life, Kati gradually became convinced that there was no future for her in Budapest. A confluence of factors prompted Kati to explore options for a new, permanent "home" – disdain toward the country that murdered her parents and nearly took her own life, recurring experiences of social exclusion within the family home as well as at school, and feelings of helplessness contributed to Kati's decision to seek refuge outside of post-war Hungary. Also contributing to this decision was her beloved Aunt Margaret's refusal to support her education beyond the eighth grade. Margaret preferred that her teenaged niece become a businesswoman and help her run the family's poultry stand. A move to Palestine was out of the question. Despite the ideological indoctrination received at the orphanage and the recognized need for a Jewish homeland, Kati refused to enter another war zone.

Staff at the local office for the humanitarian aid organization the American Jewish Joint Distribution Committee, known to Kati and other survivors simply as the Joint, presented Kati with another option.[3] As healthy Jewish orphans under the age of eighteen, they were eligible to apply to immigrate to a free country where they would have the opportunity to continue their education and be adopted together by a Jewish family. With little knowledge of the country beyond the vastness of its geography, distance from Europe and English-speaking population, Kati selected Canada as the preferred site of resettlement. Ilonka's desperation to stay with her sister – convinced that a better life waited on the other side of the Atlantic Ocean – superseded her own desire to remain with relatives in Hungary.

Some 1,123 child survivors immigrated to Canada on the War Orphans Project. Planning for the refugee resettlement scheme, proposed and administered by the Canadian Jewish Congress, began in the lead-up to World War II. At that time, Canadian Jewish leaders, despite their best efforts, were unable to persuade the Canadian government to end its discriminatory and restrictive policies concerning the rescue of Jewish children trapped under Nazism. In October 1942, Frederick C. Blair, the blatantly antisemitic head of the Department of Mines and Resources (the predecessor to the Ministry of Citizenship and Immigration) begrudgingly granted permission for five

---

3 Founded in 1914, the American Jewish Joint Distribution Committee, also known as the Joint, is the leading Jewish humanitarian aid organization, serving communities in more than seventy countries around the world. After World War II, the Joint provided financial aid to surviving Jewish communities, and attended to the daily needs of refugees in post-war Europe. Joint caseworkers worked collaboratively with other refugee resettlement agencies to facilitate the immigration of Holocaust survivors to permanent sites of resettlements. See Yehuda Bauer, *American Jewry and the Holocaust: The American Jewish Joint Distribution Committee, 1939–1945* (Detroit: Wayne State University Press, 1981).

hundred Jewish children to enter Canada via Vichy France under two conditions. First, Canada's Jews needed to provide guarantees for the youngsters' maintenance and identify suitable foster homes. And second, only orphaned children of deportees, aged two to fifteen years, could apply. Blair left open a window for five hundred additional children to immigrate at a later date.[4] All efforts to implement this plan collapsed, however, with the November 1942 Allied invasion of Vichy North Africa.

Some five years later, on April 29, 1947, the government of Prime Minister William Lyon Mackenzie King approved Order-in-Council 1647.[5] This decision represented Canada's first significant effort to help alleviate the Jewish refugee crisis plaguing post-war Europe, and the liberalization of its overall immigration policies and laws. In this context, the government expanded the original War Orphans Project's parameters to include Jewish war orphans up to age eighteen in light of the fact that few "children" survived the Holocaust.[6] Canada granted all one thousand visas at once.

To qualify, child survivors needed to provide proof of age and status as a "complete orphan" and endure intensive physical and psychological examinations. On August 23, 1948, the *Aquitania*, a luxury liner commandeered to transport immigrants across the Atlantic, docked at Pier 21 in Halifax, Nova Scotia. Included on the ship's pas-

---

4   Irving Abella and Harold Troper, *None is Too Many: Canada and the Jews of Europe 1933–1948* (Toronto: Lester & Orpen Dennys Publishers, 1982), 111–117.

5   Immigration Branch, RG Vol. 477, file 739325. L A C.

6   Children, along with the elderly and the disabled, were among the earliest and most vulnerable victims of National Socialism. As many as 1.5 million Jewish children, or some 93 per cent of those living under occupation between 1939 and 1945, were murdered during the Holocaust. For a detailed account of childhood during the Third Reich, see Deborah Dwórk, *Children with a Star: Jewish Youth in Nazi Europe* (New Haven, CT: Yale University Press, 1993).

senger roster were Kati, Ilonka and some twenty other Jewish war orphans, destined for new lives throughout Canada.[7]

Assigned the Anglicized names Kitty and Ellen by a Jewish Family and Child Services social worker, the sisters saw their high expectations crushed. At the temporary housing centre in Toronto where the girls awaited their next steps, the subject of an adoptive family for the sisters did not arise; instead, comments about "paid homes," separation and "upkeep" were voiced. The hot and humid climate, so different from the cold temperatures the girls anticipated, and the "overgrown village" feeling of Toronto convinced the girls that life in Canada might not have been everything they had hoped it would be. Culture shock, language barriers and the trauma of being separated once again plagued the girls and shaped their experiences of resettlement and integration in Canada.

Their fates determined by the pen stroke of the social worker assigned to their files, the teenaged Hungarian war orphans struggled to align their dual identities: as survivors of trauma, lacking the agency or ability to express their feelings, experiences or needs; and as "new Canadians," expected to shed their pasts and integrate seamlessly into their new homes and homeland. All the while the girls, like other war orphans, felt obliged to behave obediently in relation to their guardians or keepers, regardless of the treatment rendered.

The sisters felt misled by the Joint's promise of a loving adoptive

---

7 On the War Orphans Project, see Ben Lappin, *The Redeemed Children: The Story of the Rescue of War Orphans by the Jewish Community of Canada* (Toronto, ON: University of Toronto Press, 1963); Adara Goldberg, *Holocaust Survivors in Canada: Exclusion, Inclusion, Transformation, 1947–1955* (Winnipeg, MB: University of Manitoba Press, 2015); Fraidie Martz, *Open Your Hearts: The Story of the Jewish War Orphans in Canada* (Don Mills, ON: Véhicule Press, 1996); and *Open Hearts – Closed Doors: The War Orphans Project*, an online exhibit from the Vancouver Holocaust Education Centre, hosted by Virtual Museum Canada: http://www.virtualmuseum.ca/sgc-cms/expositions-exhibitions/orphelins-orphans/english/

home. Kati/Kitty, for her part, endeavoured to advance beyond the card originally dealt to her and reinvented herself in a stable and caring home environment. Ilonka/Ellen, lonely and fearful, suffered mainly in silence, closeting her experiences from new friends and later, after leaving school, colleagues. Instead of relying on foster parents for love and support, she developed coping mechanisms and harnessed her inner compass, leaning on only herself and her sister and teachers for guidance.[8] This strength, harnessed from early childhood memories, was a constant companion for the girls during their first years in Canada.

A story of courage, loss and an unbreakable bond between sisters, the memoir sheds important light on child survivors' resilience and tenacity in "starting over" after the Holocaust. "I firmly believe our lives must have purpose and that we need to be creative, unafraid of new beginnings and opportunities, and keep on living and growing, firmly rooted to the ground," Ellen wrote about her and Kitty's channelling of their traumatic experiences to ultimately thrive in their adopted country. The resettlement and integration experiences of Kitty and Ellen, along with those of 35,000 other Holocaust survivor immigrants and War Orphans, provide an opportunity for Canadians to critically reflect on treatment of refugees and displaced persons today. While we cannot turn back the clock to correct the missteps of the past, lessons gleaned from this historical incident might ease the journeys of new refugees desperately searching for "home."

Dr. Adara Goldberg
2015

---

8 Dr. Robert Krell, "Hiding During and After the War," in Dr. Robert Krell, ed., *Childhood Survivors: Memories and Reflections* (Victoria, BC: Trafford Publishing, 2007), 33–39.

Map

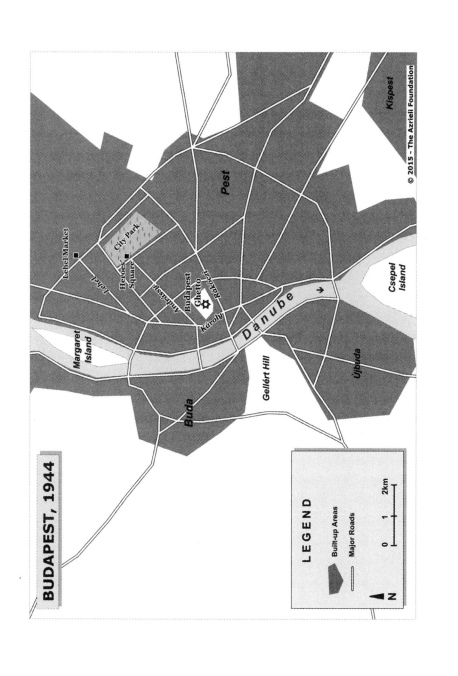

BUDAPEST, 1944

Kispest

Pest

City Park

Lehel Market

Lehel

Heroes'
Square

Andrássy

Budapest
Ghetto

Rákóczi

Károly

Csepel
Island

Danube

Margaret
Island

Buda

Gellért Hill

Újbuda

LEGEND

Built-up Areas

Major Roads

0   1   2km

N

We dedicate this book to our parents, Borishka Federer and Marton Mozes Nagy, who never knew their little girls survived and did not get a chance to see them grow up.

Kati: An Adventure Begins

The *Aquitania* sailed majestically across the Atlantic Ocean in the blazing August sun. It was 1948, and among the ocean liner's guests was a motley crew of young people aged ten to eighteen, gathered from Europe by the Canadian Jewish Congress as some of the few surviving, parentless children of the Holocaust.[1] Not only had finding them been difficult, but also having Canada accept them, since the Canadian government's antisemitic policies toward Jews and immigration had only just begun to change.

I was on that ship, among those young people, along with my thirteen-year-old sister, Ilonka. Oblivious that I was admitted to Canada only because it was embarrassing for the government to say no – although I believe it had kept stalling, trying to make some of the children ineligible because they had reached the age of eighteen – I was ecstatic to have travelled through Europe by train, stayed in a villa in France, and finally been put on an ocean liner where I ate dinners served by waiters as I sailed toward unknown adventures.

Not that I had not already had enough adventures in my short fifteen years. The earliest I can recollect is crossing a village road in

---

1 For information on the Canadian Jewish Congress, as well as on other major organizations; historical, religious and cultural terms; significant historical events and people; geographical locations; and foreign-language words and expressions contained in the text, please see the glossary.

Hungary while holding on to my little sister's hand as we carefully avoided the ferocious geese ready to attack anyone entering their territory. My second is from living in a one-room basement apartment in Budapest with my parents, my sister and a newly arrived grandmother from Romania. I do not remember going to the bathroom there, perhaps because we did not have one. I now know that among all the humiliating experiences my well-brought-up mother had to endure – aside from battling the bedbugs that infested this windowless hovel in the worst district of the city – was carrying out the chamber pots and emptying them into one of the filthy community toilets located on every floor in each corner of the large tenement building.

I do not remember any toys or games at home, nor do I recall the quarrels that took place between my mother and father, or the anger and frustration she expressed about her mother-in-law, who of course sided with her son. I think I blocked those moments out, and I only learned of them much later from my sister, who remembers them vividly and has been strongly affected by them all through her life.

I do recall feeling good about our move to a one-bedroom apartment with a cement-floored kitchen, in the same building but on the second floor. Living in the sunlight was better. In this tiny place, we still had no bathroom or electricity, although by then modern apartments in Budapest had electricity. We did have a small sink in the narrow kitchen, and a wood-burning stove for both heat and cooking. I now know that my mother needed to go into the central courtyard to chop wood for the stove just to heat some water. And now I understand why she began to cry and couldn't stop when, as she bathed me in a small washtub balanced between two chairs, I upset it when I made it rock, since to me it was a boat. But even in her despair, she did not yell at me or hit me, as many mothers did to their children in that neighbourhood. Her love surrounded me and later protected me from the degradation, trials and dangers that would come in my life.

However, for as long as I could remember, my mother, Borishka, had been depressed. I learned later that this was not always so. There was a time in her childhood, even in her teenage years, when she was a lively and attractive girl, full of anticipation for a life filled with love and beauty. She resembled my handsome grandfather the most, with her jet-black hair that contrasted her alabaster complexion, and she was his favourite. As a youngster, she teased her little sister, Margaret, with a shaming singsong she made up, which Aunt Margaret still remembered as an adult because it was so annoying. My aunt Gizi, the oldest of the three sisters, felt strong jealousy toward my mother because, as far as she was concerned, Borishka had everything and got away without punishment from their father for anything she did wrong.

My lovely mother's dreams and aspirations came to an abrupt end when, working as a secretary in an office, she met and fell in love with a young man who declared that if she did not marry him, he would kill himself. So, against her parents' wishes, she eloped with this man, who turned out to be a drunkard and a brute whose favourite pastime was beating up his young, terrified wife. Divorce, almost unheard of in those times and a terrible disgrace, was the only solution, and my grandparents insisted upon arranging it after seeing their beautiful daughter bruised and fearful time after time.

I heard that when my mother moved back in with her parents, she lost the spark she used to have. As a divorced woman, she was not considered respectable. Her older sister, Gizi, got married, as did her younger sister, Margaret, and their wedding pictures were proudly displayed in my grandparents' home. In time, Gizi bore a girl and Margaret had two boys, one after another.

My mother had started to resign herself to living out her life alone, without a husband or children, when she met the man who was to become my father. Marton was a salesman in a nightclub where Margaret's husband, Vili, was head waiter. My father was not considered a good catch since he did not have a good job or a well-established family in Hungary. He had left Romania to escape being conscripted into the Romanian army during depression times, and he had little chance of making a good living – he was earning only a modest income through his ability to sell. But he was soft-spoken, with aristocratic features and large, dreamy grey-blue eyes. He was also a bit younger than my mother, who by this time was in her late twenties. Not being a Hungarian citizen, he may have decided that it was to his advantage to be married to one.

For my romantic mother, marriage meant being loved by a handsome man and having the children she longed for. Harsh reality set in when, after having given birth to her treasured children in the midst of the depression, she did not have enough money to provide them a decent home or even adequate food. Things went from bad to worse. Not only did her husband move his mother from Romania into their crowded home, he also continued his lifestyle as a bachelor, leaving my mother with all the responsibilities.

My mother's family was loving and caring, and my grandparents, Aunt Margaret, and Uncle Latzi, my mother's younger brother, were protective and supported her. Only Aunt Gizi was different. She had married a very nice man, also called Latzi, and they were bringing up their only child, Magda, to be a lady. Magda wore lovely clothes and had lots of toys, including a porcelain-faced doll, which I inherited and promptly broke by accident. They lived in a clean apartment building in a good neighbourhood, and although they had only a kitchen and a large bed-sitting room, as did most average-income city families at that time, their home was beautifully furnished and had a baby grand piano.

Magda played the piano. When I reached the age of seven, my mother took me to my aunt Gizi's home because my mother thought it would be good for me to start learning to play piano. She thought this was not too much to ask of Gizi, since Gizi was already teaching piano to my cousin Hedi, who was a year younger than I was. Aunt Gizi's way of teaching included smacking my fingers every time I played a wrong note, and she told my grandparents, in front of me, that little Hedi was much more talented than I was. She also treated my mother and me differently from other visitors. I did not notice this until one day, as I waited for my lesson while sitting in Gizi's kitchen with my mother and my sister, a lady dropped in and Gizi promptly escorted her into the more elegant bed-sitting room to be entertained, while leaving us sitting in the kitchen, waiting.

~

At home, often after I fell asleep, my father would wake me to give me dates and sweets from the nightclub where he worked selling perfumes to the ladies and prophylactics to the men. My younger sister would be woken up for treats, too, but in the morning when I reminded her of how good they tasted, she often cried because she did not remember.

My father was tall and handsome, and he had an air of mystery about him, because even though he was considered Jewish, he had an unusual Hungarian name. His birth name in Romania was Marton Nagy. But once in Hungary, he was registered as Mozes-Nagy Marton, since in Hungary the given name is placed after the family name. His mother's maiden name was Regina Herschkovich, which was a common name for Jewish families in Arad, Romania, and his father's family name was Nagy, a common Hungarian name. My father told us that after his father died at the age of thirty-six during World War I, he had to go live in an orphanage because his mother could not support him on her own and she had no family to help. Since my dad's mother was Jewish, he was placed in a Jewish orphanage, where it was the practice to give boys with no Hebrew name the name Moses. I think that is how he became Mozes Nagy in Romania. He was a charming, gentle and peaceful man, and he certainly did not wish to die in a war as his father had, so he ran away to Hungary to escape such a fate. In Hungary, the name Mozes was mistakenly considered part of his family name. This is how, I believe, he got a hyphenated name, part Jewish and part Hungarian.

After my father married my mother, he was able to bring his

mother – whom we all called Mutter, the German word for mother – from Romania. To me she seemed strange, and I think she may have had the beginnings of dementia. My father displayed his love for her in the way he cared for her. He bathed her and even cut her toenails, with as much tenderness as my mother showed Ilonka and me. Mutter lived with us in the crowded little apartment for only a short while. She slept on a cot in the kitchen until my father found more appropriate accommodations for her. I think Mutter must have suffered greatly, not only because of the move from one country to another, but also because of the strong resentment and frustration my mother demonstrated for having to accommodate the confused old lady. It was tragic for both of them to be thrown together by circumstance, with each powerless to change the situation. When I think of this grandmother, so small and frail, I think of the plight of many old ladies in the world who no longer have protection or hope or love at the end of their lives.

My father was a very good salesman. I am sure being handsome, smart and well spoken were to his advantage in his business. He was also quite resourceful. He would do magic tricks at the nightclub to attract an audience. Once everyone felt entertained and in a good mood, he had an easy time finding customers for the things he sold. I had fun watching him practise his magic tricks at home. He also sang songs to me, which I still remember, although I cannot recall any conversations my father and I must have had. He taught me lots of songs, and sometimes he would take me with him to the nightclub and put me on a table, where I would dance and sing, charming all the people who had gathered around. I guess I was an alternative to the magic tricks.

On the nights that my dad took me out to show me off as competition to Shirley Temple, he also took me to the apartment of a friendly lady. I later learned she was his mistress. I did not, of course, realize that the reason the money he earned for rent and food was so scarce was because it was divided between the friendly lady and our family.

As far as I was concerned, my father was the most wonderful in the world. He was the dad who did magic, sang funny songs and brought me treats in the middle of the night. My mother, on the other hand, was not so much fun, though I could always count on her unconditional love and selfless care.

Soon after those visits to the friendly lady, I was moved – without any explanation – to my mother's parents' one-bedroom apartment. I slept in the middle of my grandparents' large double bed. My grandfather's head was at the headboard, my grandmother's at the other end, and I was snug in the middle, kicking Grandpa, or so he said, and wetting their bed.

I did not see my mother, my father or my sister for quite a while. My mother was a well-qualified secretary and she had taken a job. With my father and Ilonka gone from my life, I was now entertained by my grandfather, Ignace Federer. He played the violin for me in the dark kitchen, and I had fun helping him organize coins to take to the bank. I was even allowed to get him a large mug of beer from the corner pub every so often, which I then carried back to the apartment building, carefully licking off the foam.

Then, suddenly, I found out what happened to Ilonka. I was in the middle of washing myself, busily using a large washbowl but listening intently to every word my grandparents spoke to each other. They said my parents had rushed to the countryside, where they had left their four-year-old with some people who looked after children so the parents could work. My mother and father were extremely alarmed when they were notified their little girl was close to death from dysentery. The crisis of trying to save Ilonka brought my parents together again. I was only a child, but I understood that my baby sister, who was my constant admirer, could be dead. I remember visualizing her baby face surrounded by soft curls, and silently crying into the washbowl.

Then, miraculously, we were all back together in our tenement apartment, except that my father's mother was no longer there. I did not care; I did not miss her. She didn't dress nicely like my other grandma, Franceska, who put on lipstick and a pretty dress when she took me to the light comedy shows some weekends or to visit a friend who was a retired opera singer. All Mutter had done was sit in the kitchen, not saying or doing much of anything, while my mother yelled at her. In any case, I was happy to be back in my home, with my father singing me funny songs, my little sister pestering me to tell her stories and my mother catering to my sister's every whim or walking me back and forth to my first year in grade school.

School was a glorious place. I picked up reading easily and had a ferocious appetite to read more and more. My mother was proud of me, and my uncle's wife, Serena, was jealous, because although her little girl, Hedi, was much prettier than I was and just as smart, I was still my grandparents' favourite. This happiness, however, did not last long.

Ilonka: A Younger Sister's Memories

I am like the Joshua tree that grows in the Mojave Desert. It stands firmly in the ground, through hot days and cold nights, surviving the harsh dryness with hardly a drop of water and withstanding the cruel winds that batter it. No matter what, it lives on, grounded.

Like that tree, my life started in a desert. My desert was the political climate of Nazism, amid economic depression. But how I reacted to the events that tried to destroy my life was strongly influenced by my parents' overwhelming love, which was a protective force. I absorbed their love and hopes for me into the essence of my being. Their influence was imprinted on my mind and moulded it, leaving me with trust and love in spite of everything. During the cruel winds of hatred when I was left alone, deprived, scared and lonely, I cannot say I emerged without emotional scars, but the roots of my being, my attitudes and concepts about the basic goodness of human beings, kept me grounded, determined not to give up but to live on and keep growing.

The Joshua tree's life expectancy is long. When the time comes to blossom, the tree sends out shoots from each branch and displays gorgeous flowers in a variety of colours, depending on the species. A last hurrah, for the flowers wilt! But they drop their seeds for the winds to bury in the earth. My deeds and thoughts are the seeds of my life, and I believe that as I share them, they will grab hold in my children, and my spirit of endurance will triumph and continue through them.

The Joshua tree is serene. It accepts the order of the universe – birth, life and death – as nature takes over. Like the tree, I too stand still, overlooking the scenes of my life, and marvel at its mysteries. I firmly believe our lives must have purpose and that we need to be creative, unafraid of new beginnings and opportunities, and keep on living and growing, firmly rooted to the ground.

It is not true that children get over the problems they are exposed to because they do not fully understand them, and that as children grow, they will forget about them. When children are exposed to fear, pain, injustice and ridicule, they may be affected even more powerfully, for life, because they cannot speak up for themselves and are powerless to change things.

~

In 1939, when I was about four, my Romanian grandma, Mutter, moved in with us and life at home became hell. Now, I think she had the beginnings of Alzheimer's. When I saw my daddy give her a bath in a wooden tub, she looked withered and old, her eyes vacant. My father was gentle and kind to her. She was always arguing with my mother, and Mama could not stand her. I was scared of Mutter's weird behaviour.

I got some relief from being with her when I was five years old, when my mom signed me up for kindergarten. At school, I loved the toys that were kept in the glass cabinet. There were lots of dolls, building blocks and horses, which were really only canes with plastic horses heads that had big eyes and teeth. Every boy got one, and the boys would form a circle and gallop around and around, the canes between their legs as they pretended to ride. The girls could let their imaginations run wild and play Mommy with the big rag dolls, which had red lips and buttons for eyes. I would have liked to play not only with the dolls and blocks but also with the wooden horses. Still, I was happy at playtime, because at home I had no toys at all.

During lunch period, we would open the brown bags with our names on them and eat the sandwiches we had brought. The teacher played her violin while we ate, walking slowly among us. When she saw any of the kids use their left hand to eat, she'd whack the bow on their hand to make them change to the right hand. I was scared whenever lunchtime arrived because I never knew which hand was left or right. My hands would sweat whenever the teacher came near me. I got whacked every day. At home I started to pee my pants from fear. When I told my mother what was going on, she kindly bought me a bracelet to wear so I'd know which hand to use, but I was still confused. Was I supposed to use the hand with the bracelet or the hand without it? Not knowing brought on panic and a fear of getting whacked again.

Even though I am almost two and a half years younger than my sister, Kati, I remember more about our life with my parents than she does. She mostly ignored everything around her and kept her nose in books. But I well remember going around the corner with my mother to a store in a basement where fresh straw was sold so we could fill up our potato-sack mattress, which had a slit in the middle so we could stuff it. We also bought coal and chopped wood, which we would carry home on our backs. When I got a bit older, we moved up to the second floor and were better situated. Even though we were still crowded, with no privacy, we now had both a kitchen and a room. We even got frames on which to place our mattresses, although we still could not afford ones with springs and cotton filling.

Perhaps my father grew tired of hearing the quarrels between his mom and his wife, the noisy kids and his wife's complaints about not being able to feed us better food. He got a mistress and came home quite late every night. Exceedingly lonely, my mom cried a lot. She and my father had loud arguments that left us kids scared. We loved them both. Mom was very loving toward us, and so was our dad. They both sang to us, and when we learned the songs, they would clap to show their delight. We knew they were extremely proud of us. Many people think that just because children do not say much, they do not record important things in their memories. Along with the love my parents showed Kati and me through their hugs and kisses, I quietly stored many other memories. Because we had no privacy whatsoever, I saw my father using the chamber pot in the middle of the night. While he was standing there, I pretended that I was sleeping, but I took in all the details of the procedure – and his different plumbing from mine.

Then Grandma Mutter's mental health got even worse, and she was put into a facility. This was a relief for us all at home, and gave us some peace and quiet for a while. But things didn't really change between my parents. Once, my daddy took me to a movie with his mistress, Dezsoné. I sat in the dark movie house with them and wondered why my mommy was not with us, too. They bought me a big orange to eat. I had never seen an orange or eaten one. I found it delicious, and I saved the peel.

I loved and admired my big sister, Kati. She read fairy tales devotedly and would often read out loud to me so I could enjoy the stories, too. But if I pestered her, interrupting her by asking too many questions about the princess – whether she had long hair or what colour eyes she had or if she had a dress down to the floor – Kati would get mad and stop telling me the story, and I would never find out the end of the tale. Frustrated, I would begin fighting with her, and our mother would have to separate us.

On Mother's Day, I went to my sister's graduation from Grade 1. Kati was a very good student. On stage in a pretty pink dress, she sang in Hungarian along with her classmates: "Mommy dearest, Mommy sweetest, for you are all the flowers from the garden. Yours are our kisses, the love in our hearts, and we bless your name in our prayers." Some of the children threw flowers toward their mothers. I picked up an armful and brought them to my mother, who had tears of joy in her eyes, and I was happy.

We did not have much food in our home. As far as I remember, my mother cooked only one type of food: beans. One day, we had beans with garlic, another day beans with onion and vinegar, a third day beans with tomato sauce, the fourth day beans with onion, garlic and celery. I had a constant stomach ache, and gas, gas, gas. My mother tried to make me comfortable by heating up a pot lid, putting dishtowels around it and laying it on my tummy to ease the pain.

When I began to grow more independent, my mother would send me to the store that was next to our building. She would give me a bottle for the grocery lady to put vinegar in to flavour our beans. The grocery lady used a funnel to fill up the bottle. I drank a quarter of it by the time I got home. It tasted like pickles, which I still love. Sometimes my mom would reward me by giving me the change – two or three pennies. Delighted, I would run back to the store to buy a sweet, white block of potato candy. Although I wanted to take big bites and chew it, I licked it slowly instead, to make it last longer. I loved sweets, and just like the other kids in my neighbourhood, I would pick up the dried carob pods that fell off the trees. We would chew them, swallow the sweet juice and spit out the brown seeds. One day, I saw a dog pee on them under the tree. I stopped eating them after that.

We lived across the street from a barracks where soldiers were stationed. As children, we watched how some older girls made eye contact with the soldiers and talked with them. Some of the prostitutes made more than just eye contact with them against the brick walls. I remember that once when I was walking with my mother along the soldiers' barracks, I picked up a white balloon and started to blow it up. My mother smacked it out of my hand and threw it away. I was hurt, and cried. It was mine. I had found it. My mother seemed upset, too. She kissed me later. She looked really sorry.

With not enough money for food for us and my father getting home later and later each night, my mother was crying a lot. And when my father *was* at home, he and my mother would fight loudly, throwing things at each other violently, while I, hearing everything, pretended to be asleep. Then one day all the fighting stopped. My sister was sent to my mom's parents, my father moved in with his mistress and I was put in a frightening place far from home, where I was with other children in a day and night nursery. When my parents came to visit me, they found me near death, with a fever high enough to make me delirious. They were shocked into reconciliation, and decided to live together again.

Kati and I, back together with our parents, pretended that nothing had happened, and life, such as it was, continued. I now went to grade school, learned to read and found out that in some areas I was much better than Kati. I had fun creating things with my hands. I could fold paper into different objects: a boat, a hat, an airplane. I used to cut out dolls from paper and make dresses for them, but best of all, I learned to crochet. Kati was in Grade 3, and all the girls in that class had to learn to crochet to prepare for their future lives as domestics and housewives. Kati was making a little square sampler, but she struggled with the ins and outs of the string and the crochet hook. Dejectedly, she would bring home her sweaty, dirt-covered sampler, and I would easily crochet line after line for her to take back to the teacher and show as her own work. I was ecstatic that I finally knew how to do something better than Kati did.

On weekends we would all go to Grandma Franceska and Grandpa Ignace's apartment. It was pleasant visiting them. Grandma Franceska smelled nice from her face powder and lipstick. Whenever we came, she put lots of food on the table, which all tasted good. She never burned anything like my mom did. Grandpa had a moustache, and he smelled from the cigars that he liked to smoke. He used to go into the kitchen and play the violin. As a young boy in the countryside, he had learned to play from the Roma, then called Gypsies.

Grandma had pretty china cups and made a German coffee cake called *kuglóf*, which was sweet and tasty. I loved playing with the large Harlequin doll in a fancy silk suit that decorated my grandparents' bed. Occasionally, I would twist his leg just to see it twirl, and sometimes I would worry that his leg might come out of its socket. I felt that I might have hurt him a lot.

On the weekends, my aunts and uncles also came over, along with my cousins Hedi, Imre and baby Gyurika, and we children put on shows for the adults. Kati would dance as a Cossack, crouching, then kicking out her legs, while we accompanied her performance by singing and clapping in rhythm. Then Hedi would do something to impress everyone, while I hid behind the bed, waiting to make my grand entrance, and then I would sing, to the admiration of all the grown-ups.

Not all my memories at Grandma and Grandpa's place were as wonderful. Aunt Margaret and Uncle Vili lived in the next apartment with their teenage sons, Rudi and Tibi. Rudi had a cruel streak in him, and when no one was looking, he teased and tormented me. Because my ears stuck out and I was skinny, he used to call me "Big Ears," "Rattle Bones" and "Little Stupid." He would pinch my bum while lifting my skirt and he enjoyed it when I yelled at him in my small, lisping voice to stop making fun of me. To make me feel even worse, he would mock my complaints in the same way I lisped. Nobody thought to protect me from him. I still remember the one day he farted under the blanket and then pushed me under it to breathe the fumes. His younger brother, Tibi, did not help. He laughed while I was teased, although he was really a much kinder boy. Tibi, when he was on his own, put together a radio and taught himself to speak English by listening to it.

Aside from cousin Rudi, my visits to my grandparents' place were filled with happy experiences. I got mad at my grandfather only once. He took me to his barber, who gave me a haircut that made me look like a boy. The haircut was embarrassing and I felt ugly. But I forgave Grandpa when he also took me with him to the stable he rented for his horse and he let me sit on the wagon, which was used to carry ice during the summer. I saw the horse pee, which was fascinating. It happened just like with Daddy's penis. I guess the horse must have been a boy. Grandpa's horse had a long tail that he hit flies with when they landed on his buttocks. I also found out that horses fart, too, just like cousin Rudi.

I had happy times at home as well. In our neighbourhood, we did not have lots of trees or other vegetation like the children in the countryside did, so it was a thrill to grow a bean in a pot by our window. I was captivated by the miracle of life the first time I saw a little green shoot appearing, pushing through the dark dirt, looking for sunshine and later unfolding its tiny leaves.

My parents knew it would be good for us to be closer to nature to get fresh air and sunshine. I am not sure how they managed this financially, but they sent Kati and me to summer camp. It was a mistake – we were too young to be away from our parents overnight and far away from home. A counsellor slapped Kati for wetting the bed and I was bullied. Children belong with their mothers at that age. They need protection because they can be easily victimized and tormented by older children. If the victims tell, they can be subjected to more humiliation and have to endure further suffering. I still painfully remember the injustice of the counsellor putting me in the corner to punish me for telling. I spent three weeks at that summer camp. I felt safe again when I was back in my own home and all my discomforts centred on the chicken pox.

~

My little haven was destroyed when my father, who had left his home in Romania because he did not want the regimentation of army life, was called into the slave labour section of the Hungarian army. At first, we got postcards from Daddy once in a while. He was not supposed to say where he was stationed, but Daddy had a secret code with Mommy to let us know where he was. For example, he asked how our uncle Ulrich – who was imaginary – was, which meant that he was heading toward the Ukraine. Winters there were very cold. He was supposed to remove the land mines that had been hidden by the enemy, so the soldiers would not get blown up into pieces. But once he was stationed in the Ukraine, we never heard from him again. We were hoping that he had been captured by the Soviets, but more likely he was killed by one of the explosives or by his sadistic commander, who thought it was okay for a Jew to die.

With my father gone, my mother had to make ends meet for food and rent. She found a job to do at home, stuffing plastic toy bears. She also put a bed in the kitchen and rented it to a woman with a baby. I think that poor woman, who worked as a streetcar conductor, had even more problems than we did: she did not even have her own place to live. The baby cried a lot, but they just slept there during the night. My mother also rented out my father's bed to two men from a village who had jobs at a factory in the city during the day. These men had better food than we did. I kept watching them eat bacon and eggs and potatoes. The food smelled so good. Sometimes, if I made them feel uncomfortable by standing there too long, watching them eat, they would give me some.

Kati knew nothing about these people, or about the humiliation that our mother must have felt at the lack of privacy. Because my sister was sick, she was sent to live with our grandma Franceska. I thought that Kati had influenza because she went to the library in the rain. But it wasn't influenza; it was the beginning of tuberculosis. She had to stay away from me so I would not catch it. She just ate and drank and stayed in bed, and read fairy tales all the time. So lucky, I thought.

I couldn't go to see my sister and I missed her. Now we were living a lonely life apart. I made friends with Marika, a girl about my age in the next apartment. We played together, but when she got mad at me, she called me a "Dirty Jew." It hurt me. She said I killed Jesus. I told my mom and cried, "I didn't – I didn't!" My mom hugged me and rocked me for a while until my pain subsided. I wanted to hurt Marika back, so one day I got up enough courage and yanked at her long thick pigtails, then ran up the stairs like the devil was chasing me. I locked my door so she could not get me – by that time, my mother often had to leave me on my own with a key on a string around my neck.

But Marika got even. On a cold winter day when people everywhere sat around their pot-bellied stoves to defrost their thoroughly chilled bones, we invited her over. Mommy was reading us a story from *Grimm's Fairy Tales* as we sat around our stove, which was full of crackling fire from the coal and wood and made the room warm and cozy. Marika let out a tremendous fart – I guess she had to eat beans, too – and blamed it on me. My mom got angry because we had to open the window to air out the room. The cold air came in and warm air went out with the fart. She sent Marika home. Marika and I eventually reconciled because we had no other girls our age to play with, but we never invited her over again.

Once, when I was alone at home, I got into trouble with a neighbour lady who also left her son home alone. She had wanted a daughter but had a son instead, and his bright, carrot-coloured hair grew down to his shoulders in golden red locks that would shine in the sun. He was made fun of by the other boys in the tenement because he looked like a girl. That day, I told him to come upstairs and I said, "Let's play barber." Just as I snipped one side of his golden red locks up to the earlobe, his mother, who had come home, called for him. He left in a hurry, with his half-finished haircut. Seconds later, I heard a blood-curdling scream. It scared me so much I crawled under my mother's bed, shivering, and stayed there until she got home. Even after that, for a long time I was too frightened to leave the apartment, in case I would run into that boy's mother.

My fears did not diminish. It did not help that my mother warned me never to go down to the basement, where the coal was kept. Everybody knew that the young girl who had gone down there to get coal was followed by a man who raped her and left her there bleeding. She was found alive but hysterical.

When I was just turning eight, in February 1943, I was traumatized by a tragedy I witnessed. A young man whose love for a girl was rejected jumped to his death off the third floor of the tenement into the courtyard. I saw him fly past my apartment door and land below in the snow, his neck broken. I saw his red blood painting the snow.

It also did not help my fears that it was unsafe to walk home from school without my mother's protection because small groups of anti-semitic kids ganged up on the Jewish kids and tormented them, calling them "Dirty Jews" and all kinds of other slurs. I wondered, if there is God, why does he let us suffer? I was a good little girl. I tried to show my teachers that I was nice and obedient. Making an effort to please everyone was my way. But still nobody played with me. I no longer liked going to school; without my sister as my companion and without friends, I was always sad and lonely. Even Marika, my Christian playmate, would not play with me anymore.

Kati: A Lonely Life Apart

On September 1, 1939, Germany occupied Poland and World War II was declared. In a supposed effort to right the wrongs against it from the past, Germany had already conquered Czechoslovakia, and proceeded to conquer France and many other countries. Hungary became Germany's ally in the fall of 1940. I knew nothing about this as a child, but I did know that it seemed as though everybody thought the Jews were very bad people and should not get away with all the terrible things they were assumed to have done. I knew this because in the newspapers I saw the caricatures of those big-nosed, curly-haired, evil-looking people who mocked all the "true" Hungarians. The funny thing was that until then I had hardly known that my family and I were Jewish. Unlike some folks who were observant, we were just ordinary people who did not have any special celebrations, although I sure would have liked to celebrate Christmas, for the presents under the evergreen trees and the candies hung from them.

I soon found out that I was Jewish because the kids on the street chased me with sticks and yelled "Dirty Jew!" as I ran away. My mother walked me to and from school all the time, so I would be safe. But real danger came more from the grown-ups than from the kids. Hungary began to enact many of the laws the Nazis advocated. It supported the German army with its own army, and called in all able-bodied men to serve their country. In 1940, my father was one of those able-bodied men. But, whereas gentile men were given guns for fighting, my father and other Jewish boys and men were assigned to serve troops any way the person in charge thought they would be of use. After the war, I heard that the person in charge of my father's forced labour unit in the Ukraine was a cruel man who did not hesitate to have the Jews go ahead of the gentile soldiers to look for hidden, unexploded mines. My father always thought he would die at the age of thirty-six, just as his father had. And after two years at the front, in 1942, my mother got a letter that my beloved father had disappeared. He had just turned thirty-six.

I did not fare well at the news. I stopped eating, although my mother did practically everything to make me happy, especially since I had developed tuberculosis, and the cure for it at that time was rest, fresh air and plenty of food. I could rest by not going to school, but fresh air and good food were scarce, since we still lived in the smoggy, industrial section of Budapest and my mother could no longer be employed by virtue of her Jewishness. She did some menial work on a foot-driven Singer sewing machine in the apartment, where a kind employer paid her minimally, under the table, per piece of completed work.

During this difficult time, my grandparents and Aunt Margaret came to my mother's rescue. Again I was placed in the care of my grandparents. I had to stay in bed all day – mostly without any company since my grandparents were also out during the day – except for occasional visits from Erwin and Helen Schlesinger, my mom's German cousins. While other children my age were in the last part of Grade 3 and then in Grade 4, I was stuck in my grandparents' apartment, trying to get well. There was not much to do but listen to classical music on the radio and explore my grandmother's cupboards, which contained quite a few sophisticated books. So, at the age of ten, I read both *David Copperfield* and the risqué story of a lady who was a so-called working girl at night. I also read Freud's theories of the id, ego and superego, and the dream revelations of sexual suppression, especially in hysterical women. My readings allowed me to vicariously experience the ways and sins of the world, and later, when I really was alone, without any family to protect me, this prompted me to be – in some respects – more cautious about boys and men, and a lot less romantic and gullible than other young girls of my generation.

The highlights during my forced separation from my mother and sister were the visits by cousins Erwin and Helen. Those times helped lift the boredom. Their late father, Maurice, was my grandmother Franceska's brother. He was a budding actor in Leipzig when he and a young German girl named Ida fell in love and married. Ida's family, learning of her marriage to a Jew, no matter how assimilated, excluded her and their three children from their family for the disgrace.

Unfortunately, Maurice was conscripted into the German army in World War I and was killed. Ida then brought up the children, Erwin and twins Rosa and Helen, the only way she knew: Christian, of course. When the children were in their late teens and early twenties, Ida died – just at the time Hitler and the Nazi government rose to power. Then, looking through their mother's papers, they discovered they were half-Jewish, and even though they knew nothing about religion except praying in a church to Jesus, they became undesirable and unemployable because of their "tainted blood." They also found out that their father's sister – my grandmother – was in Hungary. Franceska was more than delighted to have her brother's children visit her. And so Rosa, Helen and Erwin arrived in Hungary. Then Rosa went back to Leipzig because she had a sweetheart, Walter, waiting for her. Erwin and Helen remained in Budapest and, as Germans, were able to work.

During my long confinement, gentle cousin Erwin taught me to play gin rummy, still the only card game I know. Later, and I am not aware why, Helen came to live with my grandparents, and though she was my cousin, because of the age difference between us, as well as the warm nurturing she gave me, I called her my aunt. Auntie Helen slept on the couch at the foot of the double bed in the cramped bed-sitting room, while I continued to sleep between Grandpa and Grandma – but no longer wet their bed. Auntie Helen was lots of fun. Just like my father, she taught me to dance and sing, except the songs were in German. Then, miraculously, I got better. The X-rays showed that the dark shadows on my lung had disappeared.

My mother, at this time, could barely earn enough money for rent, so she rented out the second bed in her tenement apartment. I found this out a half century later from my quite secretive sister, who was an adult when she finally told me. The tenant fell in love with my mother. My mother once asked me what I thought of her getting married and us living in the country, where there was lots of fresh air. Why she, an adult, consulted a ten-year-old, I do not know, but I reacted decisively. I threw away the ice cream cone she had just bought me and asked her how she could think of getting married to a common peasant (though I had never even met the man) after my wonderful father! To my later regret and chronic guilt for many years, she decided not to marry the man, forfeiting her chance to get out of Budapest with her children. I felt responsible for her tragic decision. Of course I now know it was not my fault, but for a long time I thought that if only I had given her permission to remarry, people in the countryside would have known her only as the wife of this man, and that might have saved her life.

Perhaps the existence of this man was the reason I remained with my grandparents, in whose home there was always plenty of food, since Grandma Franceska and Aunt Margaret worked in an open-air market. My grandmother, an educated lady, was the real breadwinner in her family. She had been forced to work and support her four growing children after her husband was conscripted into the army during World War I. Later, when my grandfather came back from the war, he started his own transport business with horses and a wagon, but he kept the money to spend on himself and his pleasures.

Neither squeamish nor proud, Franceska owned a little poultry stall in the Lehel food market of Budapest. She, and later Margaret as well, got up early each morning, in all kinds of weather, to meet the country folk who provided plucked chickens, ducks and geese for my grandmother to sell in her stall. The merchants exchanged other foods too, so Aunt Margaret's family and my grandparents were never short of eggs, cheese, meat, bread or vegetables. I am sure they supplied food to my mother as well, while they were still allowed to own the stall.

Even though I had missed much schooling, I was allowed to enter Grade 5. I was happy to be among children once more, although I do not recall having any friends. But I did not care. I could again walk outdoors, and learn from the teacher who enriched our studies with her interests and knowledge in early Hungarian-Mongolian culture. I was a good student in languages and music, but I was awkward physically, perhaps because of my long confinement with TB, and I was behind in arithmetic; all the children had learned their times tables in Grades 3 and 4. I was in an all-girls school, where we were addressed by our last names. I hated to be called Mozes because the name was recognized as Jewish and, therefore, negative. My classmates laughed at me.

We all had to be respectful toward our teachers and we all wore the same uniform. The boys were taught separately, in another part of the building with its own entrance, and they were disciplined more harshly than the girls. In addition to the introduction of German into the curriculum, there was a class in religious education every week. When a Catholic priest came to teach catechism, I and a few other girls were sent to another classroom to learn how to be Jewish. As I left the room, complying unquestioningly, I did not realize that this visible exclusion for religious reasons may have been a part of why I was not befriended at school. It was a lesson for both the Jewish and the Catholic students that being "one of them" meant "not being one of us."

Once that school year ended, the Jewish children were excluded not only from catechism classes but also from all levels of instruction in any school in Budapest. There would be no Grade 6 studies for me. And even if I had been allowed to go to school, I could not have attended. On March 19, 1944, Germany occupied Hungary. New laws soon restricted our movements and took away our property. My grandmother's open-air poultry stall closed down that spring, when the set of laws came into effect that forbade Jews to own or operate any business that should rightfully be owned by "true" Hungarians; my grandfather then also lost his horses and wagon from his transport business.

By the beginning of April, my coat had a large six-sided yellow star sewn on it to identify me as Jewish, because despite the well-publicized stereotype depicting Jews with a big hooked nose, thick lips and dark curly hair, those Jews who did not wear the attire of the ultra-Orthodox looked just like everyone else. The rules were very serious, and not obeying them resulted in terrible consequences. I knew two young sisters in our apartment building who had removed the yellow star from their coats and gone to the movies. I never saw them again, because someone at the theatre had told the authorities that the girls were Jews and had broken the law. I am not sure what happened to them, but I remember seeing their mother crying.

It was a sad time in Budapest for everyone. The whole city had to have darkened windows because the English and the Americans could bomb the buildings if lights showed their location. I was not afraid when the sirens sounded to run down to the coal cellars in the basement, in case an enemy plane dropped a bomb on us. I found the noise and people running quite interesting. Our building was never bombed, but I heard others were, and with the destruction of apartments, many people had to find new places to live. The government had a simple solution to ease the plight of people who had lost their homes in the bombings. In June 1944, a new rule appeared stating that Jewish families could not live in their own apartments because the "true" Hungarians needed them. Instead, Jews were ordered into designated buildings, often crowded into apartments with three or more families than they could hold. The removal of Jews from their homes gave homeless Hungarians adequate places to live and gained many people's approval, since it was to the Hungarians' benefit, and concentrated the remaining Jews in convenient, controllable holding areas. These Jewish buildings mostly housed women, children and the elderly, because most of the able-bodied Jewish boys and men in Budapest had already been taken away to the forced labour service, serving and supporting the soldiers fighting for the honour of their country.

My grandparents moved into a designated Jewish holding-tank building with my mother's older sister, Aunt Gizi, while I was cared for by Aunt Margaret. Her husband and two teenage sons had long ago been conscripted into forced labour. My mother and sister were living far from where I was, also in a building designated for Jews, in the same apartment as my uncle's wife, Serena, and her three children. I did not question why I was not with my mother, since I had not lived with her for many years. Aunt Margaret was a decisive person. I adored being with her, because just like my mother, she was loving, but unlike my mother, she told me lots of funny jokes. She took special care of me because she had always wanted a little girl.

I could not carry much from my grandparents' apartment to the segregated house. I took my most precious possessions: my books. I did not have many, but they were extremely important to me. The people who shared the apartment with us were kind and interesting. One of them, Eva, was the original owner of the apartment that she now shared with us and several other people. She was a slim, quiet lady, and her friend Lizette, who also lived there, was most fascinating. Lizette, even under our circumstances, curled her eyelashes and put on makeup and lipstick, and while she was doing this, she would ask me to light her cigarette. I guess I was quite unsophisticated in spite of my extensive reading, because it never occurred to me to inhale. So, unlike other kids exposed to glamorous adults who smoked, I never got addicted.

One of the great delights of my move to this apartment with Aunt Margaret was the discovery of the indoor bathroom, equipped with toilet and bathtub. When I excitedly told my aunt about it, she shushed me, and so I learned that not ever having had a bathroom of our own was not to be publicized.

In this prison – for that is what it was – the movement of the inmates was restricted by law. Jews were incarcerated in these homes day and night except for a few hours when shopping for food was allowed. Sometimes people gathered and told each other what was going on in the outside world. We heard that people had been taken in crowded cattle cars to concentration camps, where they were killed if they could not work. After October 1944, when the fascist Hungarian Arrow Cross Party came to power, we also heard that Jews were being arrested and taken to the Danube River, which ran through Budapest, shot on the embankment and thrown into the water, to be carried away. I don't know why I did not feel panicky. I suppose that at the age of eleven, one cannot imagine the true meaning of such atrocities; also, I was having a good time with my aunt Margaret in a beautiful apartment with a real bathroom. My aunt still had her connection to suppliers from the countryside, so we were not lacking food, unlike many others. She did not share with me her concern for her husband and her sons, although I am sure she had them.

Every so often, Aunt Margaret left me with the other people in the building while she went out, without any explanation. One day, I found out what she was doing when she was not with me, and to this day I think that she is one of the unsung heroines of those terrible times of persecution. She quietly told me to remove the yellow star from my coat. She then gave me two heavy bags filled with food to carry just the way she did. She and I went to the entrance of the apartment building, where the superintendent, who was both our "keeper" and a Nazi informant, happily let us out since she was receiving a huge bribe.

Aunt Margaret appeared quite self-assured as she and I walked along the streets with our heavy loads, and because she was seemingly fearless, so was I. We finally arrived at another apartment building, where we were allowed in freely, probably by another bribed superintendent, and went up to the apartment that housed, among the many occupants, my mother; my sister, Ilonka; Aunt Serena; and my three sweet, golden-haired cousins: ten-year-old Hedi, seven-year-old Imre and their eighteen-month-old baby brother, Gyurika. So this was the destination of my aunt's mysterious trips! She was knowingly endangering herself to provide food for her sister's and brother's families. I suppose that since her previous trips had been successful, she had decided that it was not too risky to take me along so that my mother could see me. My mother was very quiet during this visit.

I did not think it unusual that I went back home with Aunt Margaret instead of staying with my mother, as my sister did – after all, I had not lived with my mother for the previous two years. I did not realize, then, that this was another way that Aunt Margaret protected her emotionally fragile sister from additional stress. Besides, being with Aunt Margaret I got all the attention; not like Ilonka, who was just one of many children in the crowded apartment.

However, my enjoyment of my new-found living arrangement, immersing myself in reading and rereading my books, ended abruptly. Hungary was the last country in Europe to systematically deport people of Jewish religion or heritage, along with others deemed "undesirable." This was not an oversight. The Nazi governments of Hungary and Germany were allies, so there was no urgency to "process" the Hungarian Jews first. The strategy was to first remove all the people in the surrounding areas, let those few who escaped flee into areas not yet processed, then systematically enclose the remaining areas. With Hungary a willing ally, cooperation was assured. I would later learn that hundreds of thousands of Hungarians had been deported to Auschwitz in the spring and summer of 1944. By the time the noose finally tightened around the Jews in Budapest, it was November of 1944.

My birthday was in November. I was turning twelve, but I never knew it – celebrating birthdays was not my family's custom. At the beginning of the month, the residents of the apartment building in which I was held captive with Aunt Margaret were told that everyone must be ready, with one suitcase, by a certain time of day for transport to another location. In secret, Aunt Margaret slipped out with me and we walked to where my grandparents were now staying with my aunt Gizi. All I carried was my box of books. Aunt Margaret dropped me off and went back to be processed with all the other inmates of her building. Ours was just one of the many buildings women were now being evacuated from, to be sent on foot and later, in cattle cars, without food or water, to Austria, to work for the German war effort. Many of these forced labourers were sent to labour camps in Austria and western Hungary; others ended up in the concentration camps of Flossenbürg, Mauthausen and Sachsenhausen.

My mother's building was also called up, and women – with their children, if they had any – were collected in the courtyards. By this time it was no longer a secret what would happen. Those who could work would have a chance to survive and those who could not, including mothers not willing to be separated from their burdensome children, would likely be sent to their deaths.

My uncle Latzi was in one of the slave labour units near Budapest and got word of his wife and children's impending fate – how, I do not know. The head of his unit was a humane and compassionate man – not everyone in Hungary was bent on the destruction of the Jews. He wrote a letter of permission giving my uncle temporary liberty for special reasons, but this was no guarantee of protection if someone decided to make an example of him for being outside the confined areas for Jews. My uncle's first move, at an added risk to himself, was to go in the middle of the night to where my grandparents were and take me with him to my mother's and his wife's segregated house. There, he collected his three children and my little sister as well. I know I saw my mother, and at twelve years of age I should have remembered this, but for some reason the precious memories of her voice and touch I should so like to recall are blocked. All I know is that this was the last time I saw my mother.

My uncle walked in the cold with five children to a large building that housed many more. I think the building may have been a residential school for the deaf, because there were lots of children who did not talk but made weird noises from their throats. Everything seemed like a strange dream. I was aware only of children, with no adults in sight, although there must have been some because we were given a mattress to lie on and some food to eat. The children were all supposed to be refugees escaping the advancing front as the Soviets victoriously pushed back the Nazis and their allies. Both women and children fled the danger of being caught in the crossfire. And the women fled attacks from the soldiers – a pastime for some of them. In spite of imminent defeat, the Hungarian fascist government and its avid supporters showed no let-up in their determination to complete the job of killing all those they deemed undesirable.

Then, without any warning, all the children hiding in this building were rounded up. We were told to go to a room that served as a pantry and to take with us whatever food we could find and carry. By the time I got there, I could find only a small jar of Ovaltine, a kind of sweet powder to mix with milk. I no longer had my books, which I hadn't had time to collect when my uncle snuck me out to save me along with his children, but I was so confused by constantly moving from place to place, and knowing that not only had I lost my father but now my mother and my aunts had also been taken from me, that I did not even give my books a thought. I grabbed my sister's hand as we were lined up on the street in the freezing cold of a December night. I heard some adults whispering, "Give us the babies." My cousin Hedi, who was looking after her two younger brothers, handed over her baby brother to a woman, never to see him again. I am sure that she thought, as I did as we marched over snow-covered ground with rifle-toting guards alongside us, that we were being led to the Danube to be shot and thrown into the river.

Ilonka: In the Dark

One day I no longer had to go to school and I no longer had to be afraid of the neighbour lady. In June 1944, a law was passed that all people who were Jewish had to move into segregated apartment buildings that were only for Jews. My mother had already sewn a yellow star on my coat, and we walked to another building, where to my great delight I found my uncle Latzi's wife, Serena, and my cousins Hedi, Imre and baby Gyurika. Hedi, like her two brothers, had blue eyes and blond hair. She and I had lots of fun playing together every day. Every so often my aunt Margaret came over with some food, and one day she even brought my sister, Kati, who was never as much fun to play with as Hedi and Imre. My mother looked so happy when she saw her, and I was happy too.

What more could anyone ask for? I had my best friends playing with me every day, I never had to go to school and my mother was always at my beck and call if I needed her, because living in this new place she never had to go out, so she never left me alone in the apartment. It was a dream come true.

Soon enough, the dream turned into a nightmare. All the grown-ups became very upset. They started to pack everything they had into one suitcase. My aunt Serena sent word to her husband that our building was to be evacuated and everyone who lived there was going to a new location. My mother, too, was troubled. She did not say anything, but I could tell. To my surprise, my uncle Latzi showed up, bringing my sister with him. He said that he would take us children with him and keep us safe. I was torn from my mother and we left, walking in the darkness to a place where children were supposed to be safe.

Uncle Latzi took us to a building that had a sign with a red cross. I knew about the Red Cross. They helped people. After my uncle left us there, our heads were shaved so we wouldn't get lice, and we were shown where we could sleep on a mat in one of the large rooms, with lots of other children. We were also given something to eat, though I don't recall what. All I remember is being hungry. But I wasn't too scared, because my sister was with me, and I knew that she would make sure that I was safe. We must have been there for at least a few months. Hedi looked after her brothers, and I stayed by Kati's side all the time. It was cold there, but not as cold as outside. When it was dark, and even in the daytime, we huddled next to each other on the mat to keep warm. I don't recollect anyone playing or singing, but some of the children made scary sounds from their throats because they were deaf. I had warm enough clothes on, but my shoes had holes in them, which my mother had covered up on the inside with cardboard. This didn't matter to me until we were made to walk outdoors when men with guns came to the building. They were angry looking and had sharp bayonets attached to these guns, so they could both shoot and stab with them. The sight was threatening and frightful.

We all lined up outside in the dark. A Red Cross nurse told Hedi that she could hide our baby cousin because he had blue eyes and blond roots, he wasn't circumcised and he hadn't yet learned to talk. Hedi trusted this lady, who seemed kind, although she was a stranger to us and we never even knew her name. The lady went away with Gyurika before the soldiers could see her. Then we were marched away from the building of safety, going where, we didn't know. I held on to Kati because I had a hard time walking. The cardboard covering one of the holes in my shoes let in the slush, and when the snow stuck to it and froze, it made that shoe higher than the other. We could not stop to scrape off the ice. Hungry, scared and freezing, I marched alongside my sister, limping as if I had one leg longer than the other.

Kati: In the Ghetto

It seems that members of the Nazi-approved Arrow Cross Party had decided to march us children into an enclosed area called the ghetto. The Budapest ghetto was established on November 29, 1944, in the last months of the war, when Germany and Hungary were in a life-and-death struggle with the Allies. Nevertheless, even in those desperate times the Nazis were still determined to finish the job of killing all the Jews of Europe in a process called the "Final Solution."

To that end, they collected all the remaining Jews of Hungary, those not in hiding or protected by some neutral government like Sweden, and placed them in an area separated from the non-Jewish population. Guarding them with armed soldiers, enclosing them within stone walls and fences, the Nazis made sure that no food could go in and nobody could come out. By keeping the Jews completely cut off from the world, it was easy for the Nazis to continue moving large, defenceless groups of people from this holding tank of misery to slave labour camps, where the Jews were used, if capable, for providing much needed labour that would free up men in the general population to be soldiers.

The people remaining inside the ghetto received no humanitarian services. Surrounded by garbage and excrement, crowded together, the starved and weakened children and the elderly easily fell sick from typhoid and other diseases. Many died horribly. They were left out in the streets, or in areas not as plainly seen.

After Ilonka and I were shown to an apartment in a building, we stayed inside with one group of children, huddling because of the cold. Hedi and Imre were separated from us and put into another apartment, and I lost sight of them. Years later, I found out that my cousin Imre had decided to explore his unfamiliar surroundings. As he walked into a bombed, half-destroyed stairway, he stumbled and fell on top of a dead man. I don't think he ever got over it.

I was aware of the scary situation we were in, but unlike Ilonka, I did not feel scared. In fact, I did not feel much of anything at all, except cold and hungry. As I lay beside Ilonka, I thought of all the food I had refused to eat when my sweet and caring mother had tried to get me well, but I did not think of my father or my mother or my aunt Margaret being marched away, possibly to their deaths. I just daydreamed about food and wished that it could be warmer in the apartment in the middle of a harsh December.

I hunted around the apartment and found a closet full of abandoned clothes. Since we had no blankets, I put on layers of them and went to sleep. In the middle of the night, I awoke with a terrible itch all over my body. When daylight came and I looked at the clothes I had found, I saw they were full of bugs and eggs. That is when my feelings broke through. On my own, without adults, degraded by the filth and by the bugs that attacked my body, I bowed my shaved head in despair and started to sob uncontrollably. Then I had to stop so as not to frighten my already terrified sister.

There must have been people in the ghetto who, despite their own plight, tried to save the children from starving to death. I remember being given a metal cup filled with a thick mash of peas and beans. It was called "B. B. soup." Ilonka and I ate this soup, even though she found a worm floating on top of it. No longer squeamish or fussy, I felt my most important job was to keep my sister and myself alive. After a day or two, we no longer received any soup. I am not sure how many days we were left without any food.

The bombing was constant as the invading Soviet army drew closer and closer to Budapest. We were led out of the apartment by some
adults and told by these kind people to stay in the coal cellar of the
building. That way, we would have some protection from the collaps-
ing buildings if there was a hit. I did not worry about that, because
I knew that if we didn't get any food soon, we would surely die. I
walked around the ghetto even during those attacks, going into abandoned apartments and bombed-out stores to search for something
edible to bring to my sister, ignoring the whistling bullets and the
exploding bombs.

There wasn't much to find. I came across some chicory – a plant
root roasted and used during the war as a coffee substitute – and some
dried onion flakes in a bag, and to my joy, in a bombed-out drugstore,
I found a whole bunch of chocolates called "Ex-lax." I took all these
back for Ilonka and me to eat. She was rapidly losing her strength, or
maybe she was just discouraged, because this once happy-go-lucky
little girl who loved to play, dance and sing just lay there, waiting for
me. We were very lucky – now that I know what Ex-lax is used for –
that it had no harmful effect on us, since the drugs in it had long ex-
pired, and for a short while longer the chocolate and sugar in it gave
us some energy. Pretty soon, this too dissipated, and I no longer had
any desire to leave the cold, dark coal cellar. I just lay there with my
sister's body close to mine, among the other children who were in the
same condition we were.

As an adult, when I talked to a group of children about my childhood experiences, a young girl asked me, "What did you do? Did you
cry? Did you yell and scream? How did it feel to be dying?" I told her
that dying was not painful, nor was it full of yelling and screaming;
it was quiet. As I lay there mostly sleeping or, more likely, semi-con-
scious, I no longer felt hungry or cold. I felt nothing and thought of
nothing.

Finally, on top of all the miracles that had kept us alive until then,
came the miracle of liberation of the Budapest ghetto by the Soviet

army, just as Ilonka and I were at the threshold of death by starvation. The people of Budapest still talk about the savagery of the Soviet soldiers who defeated the Hungarians in January 1945. The soldiers robbed people, beat them, took them away as captives and brutally raped many of the girls and women. But they were wonderful to us. Kind, gentle soldiers fed my sister and me – the other children too – from their own food. Although I could not understand their language, I knew that what they were saying to us meant that we were no longer in danger and that we would live.

Ilonka: Poems

When the scary soldiers took us to our destination, which was behind a high fence, we were led to a grisly-looking building with dirty grey walls pockmarked from bullets. I saw all around me shabbily dressed, gaunt-faced strangers, some with open sores. Nobody spoke. Some of us from the group were moved into one of the apartments in the building, and when that was filled, some of the other children were moved to another vacant apartment. That is how Hedi and Imre were separated from Kati and me until we all had to go to the coal cellars in the basement to be safer from the bombs raining from the sky. I still remember the terrible feeling I had then, so when someone asked me much, much later how I felt during the Holocaust, here is what I wrote in some of my many poems as an answer:

What is it like to be a Holocaust child?
Hungry, homeless and left behind
Bewildered, abandoned, there is no one who cares
Desolate surroundings, and the winter is fierce.

I want my mommy!
Where did she go?
Soldiers with bayonets marched her away
To some place I don't know

She looked so despondent
Her spirit seemed low
Only footprints were left behind
Leaving tracks in the snow.

I want my mommy!
That is all I could think
To give me love and comfort
Food and water to drink

My needs have fallen
On cruel and deaf ears
I have had this yearning since then
All through the years.

IN THE GHETTO OF BUDAPEST

Sirens are whining that hurt our ears,
announcing arrival of enemy planes.
They drop bombs to let us know
they will conquer while we're cowed below.
Hungary is bombed day and night.
We're hiding in basements, don't see daylight.
The earth shakes each time a bomb explodes;
could be buried alive by tomorrow, who knows?
We're living in the basement among the rats and mice
Our heads have been shaved 'cause we have bugs and lice.
The future looks bleak, our hopes are almost gone,
The sirens are screaming, the bombs are coming down.
Since our heads are shaved, and we look gaunt and starved,
I want to just lie down and leave this world behind.
My sister found some scraps; she feeds them to me.

"Don't give up, Ilonka. You mean the world to me."
She is so protective, trying to do her best
To keep my spirit going, says this war can't last.
Still I want to be babied and loved, like I used to be before
But that's only a pipe dream, since our parents were killed in the war.

A DAY IN THE GHETTO'S UNDERGROUND CELLAR

Our bodies are weak from starvation,
our heads shaved to the roots
Infested conditions are hard to tolerate,
spiralling our spirits down to a depressing mood.
People around us are dropping like flies,
typhoid season arrived that is threatening our lives.
People with high fever are losing all their strength
Will we be alive tomorrow?
Rats and mice come out at night
We fear they could be rabid, and will bite us in the dark.
We don't know what the future holds; we huddle to keep warm.
I don't want to live anymore; misery has taken its toll.
Red Cross brings us meatless soup made of old peas that worms float on
I am so hungry I don't care, hoping for seconds while I may.
The winter is very cold with no heat or clean water
I never change clothes or take a bath; our feet freeze and our teeth chatter.
With blank faces and no expression, life seems hopeless and bleak
Our spirit is dying within; we have little need to speak.
Just waiting for death with all hope gone,
Curled up in a fetal position on a filthy mattress infested with bugs.
For a young child it seems like years when finally it's the end of the war
But such suffering and so much loss of lives, what was this war all for?

Kati: So Many Miracles

When I think about it, I realize that life is full of miracles. Even my existence is a miracle. Had my grandparents not made my mother's first husband divorce her, in spite of the conventions of that time, my mother and father could not have married and had Ilonka and me. It was a miracle too, as far as I am concerned, that I recovered in my childhood from tuberculosis without any treatment at a time when the science of medicine was not as advanced as it is today.

It could be called luck, but I think it was a miracle that my parents were able to snatch Ilonka back from death's door after she had been farmed out to caretakers in the countryside, and could nurse her back to health. And a miracle that Aunt Margaret and I were not discovered by the police as we carried food to my mother, either on the way to her building or on the way back. If we had been caught on the street at a forbidden time and without a yellow star on our coats, we surely would have been sent to a concentration camp or a death camp, and I, a skinny young girl, would have been murdered because that was how children were routinely dealt with at those places. How miraculous too that my uncle Latzi took an additional risk by collecting me on his way to get his own children and my sister, and because he had saved me, my sister and I were together in the ghetto and I could become her protector, such as it was, and save her in turn.

There were other miracles that saved our lives, that I found out about only much later. As I mentioned, because the Hungarians were allies of the Germans, the genocide of the Jews in Hungary was left to the end of the war, so Ilonka and I were able to lead a relatively normal life most of the time, even when the defeat of the Nazi governments of Germany and Hungary was just a matter of months away. This made it possible for us to stay with, and be protected by, the adults of our family for a longer time than were Gypsy and Jewish children in neighbouring countries in Eastern Europe. Even on our way to the ghetto we could have been shot and thrown into the Danube River by our Arrow Cross guards. Because we were defenceless children, it could have been done so easily, and it was not unusual for the Arrow Cross to dispose of many of their victims in this way.

I think too that it was miraculous that my cousin Hedi gave her baby brother to that kind lady. Although Hedi forever felt horribly guilty about not finding Gyurika ever again, I am sure that he could not have survived the harsh cold, the diseases and deprivation, for even the few weeks that we spent in the ghetto without the protection of adults, and I am certain this woman helped save his life. Then, because I was willing to forage for food among the ruins, I gave Ilonka and me a small advantage for survival.

I now know, from reading historical documents, that Adolf Eichmann had delegated a German general to massacre all the people remaining in the Budapest ghetto. Had it not been for the influence of Raoul Wallenberg, a humanitarian Swedish diplomat who talked him and his cohorts out of this scheme, that would have been the end of existence for everyone in the ghetto. In addition, my cousins, my sister and I could have died from starvation in a few more days had the Hungarians been able to hold on to their city a little longer. But, as a final miracle, we were rescued by the Soviet soldiers just in time and got another chance at life.

～

I do not remember being transported out of the rat-infested basement of that building in the Budapest ghetto. When I regained awareness, I found myself, along with my sister, in a large building, on a bed with a blanket, near a wood-burning stove radiating warmth. I must have been given food, because I had enough strength to get out of bed and walk around. During my exploration of my new surroundings, I came across a mirror on a wall. When I looked into the mirror, a stranger with a bald head, huge eyes and sunken cheeks stared back at me. I did not recognize myself.

I decided to leave the comfort of the building – maybe because I had previously emulated Aunt Margaret's courageous behaviour – and started to walk about to see what was around us, but I made sure I knew how to get back to my sister and cousins. One time, as I wandered in a nearby neighbourhood, I came across the building Aunt Margaret and I stayed in when it was a segregated house for Jews. When I recognized this building from a happier past, my apathy broke again, and I began to cry – but this time with joy.

I entered the building and knocked on the door of the apartment I had once lived in with my aunt. To my delight, Eva, who had housed us, opened the door! I think she was shocked to see me so changed in such a short time. She invited me inside, fed me and said I could take a bath in her fabulous indoor bathroom. Not only that, she said my sister was also welcome to come and bathe. I went back to lethargic Ilonka, made her climb out of bed and led her to Eva's place for a bath. By the time I got my sister to this compassionate lady, Eva had already inquired after the whereabouts of my family members, located them, and let them know we had survived and where to find us.

So this too was a miracle as far as I was concerned (even though I helped it along with my adventurous actions), because the next day my auntie Helen appeared and took the four of us to the place she was staying with our grandparents and Aunt Gizi. Auntie Helen burned our clothes but did not shave off our hair, which was just starting to grow in. Instead, she worked very hard to get rid of all the lice with

a foul-smelling petroleum. She and Aunt Gizi also made short journeys to the countryside to barter for food with the farmers to help
feed our grandparents and us. They provided everything.

My grandfather, who could not see well for as long as I could remember, was now almost totally blind; Hedi was still sick because
of starvation; and my grandmother Franceska just lay there, though
nobody explained to us why. We heard that many people who were
taken away during the Nazi regime were on their way back to re-enter
society. We were now waiting for our loved ones: Aunt Gizi's husband
and their daughter, Magda; my mother; Aunt Margaret, Uncle Vili
and their sons, Rudi and Tibi; my uncle Latzi and his wife, Serena.
Nobody thought that my father would come back, except Ilonka and
me. We never believed that our exciting, handsome, fun-loving father
could be defeated and cease to exist.

Aunt Gizi and Aunt Helen made arrangements with a health organization program to send Imre, Ilonka and me to the countryside,
which would get us out of the city and ensure fresh air and food. I
think, in the back of their minds, they also thought this would make
room in our tiny place for any of the family members they hoped
would come home soon, since so many of the slave labourers now
had their freedom back. Only Hedi was not sent away, because she
was still very sick.

Just as we were leaving for the countryside to regain our health,
to our joy Aunt Margaret's younger son, Tibi, arrived from Germany.
Unlike all the other poor souls who survived their treatment in the
Nazi camps, Tibi was not only *not* skin and bones, he was practically
fat! Not only that, he also brought with him a whole lot of food supplies for the family. He told us that at liberation he was just as thin
as the rest of the inmates in the camp, but the Americans had come
to the rescue, and he could communicate with them in English. The
Americans hired him as a kitchen boy and he had all the food that his
stomach could hold. Seeing him so well gave us all strong hope that
soon everyone would come back. So, filled with hope, I went away

with Ilonka and Imre to the countryside. I started looking forward to adventures in a new place just as any child would who had been cooped up in the segregated buildings and the awful basements of the ghetto.

I am sorry to say that I was not properly grateful to the country folk who volunteered to house and feed me. The farmer and his family were good people who said that not only would they provide me with food and shelter, but they would also give me a dress in exchange for taking their cow to the pasture. All I had to do was wait until the cow ate enough and then bring her home. Well, I never cared much for clothes, just as long as they kept me warm and had no bugs in them. Simply sitting on the grass, watching a docile cow eat, was not what I wanted to do. So after a week or so, when I had finished reading the few books that I found in their cottage – which I did quickly while watching the cow – I begged them to let me go back to the nearby city, where the children who were too young to be sent to the farms were housed. The farmer and his family were not upset, and I don't remember for sure, but I think they may even have given me the dress as wages for watching the cow.

Ilonka: Orphans

The countryside was quite a revelation for me. The roads were different from the ones in the city. They had no sidewalks, they were dusty, and in the rain they became muddy because they were unpaved. People usually walked barefoot, and when it rained, they wore boots. Instead of tall buildings, straw-roofed whitewashed houses lined either side of a road, and both the front and the backyards of the houses had trees of quite a variety. I loved that instead of carobs on which dogs could pee, these trees grew apples, pears and apricots, all of them, to my delight, edible.

I noticed other differences between the city and the county. At first I had to get used to how people talked, because even though they spoke Hungarian, it sounded different from the Hungarian we spoke in Budapest. I stayed with a kind family in a fairly large house. I think the people were quite well off, because they had lots of animals. In the barn were cows and horses, in a pen nearby were pigs, and in the yard, running around, were chickens and roosters. They had a large dog and several cats as well. One part of the yard was set aside for a small garden that grew all kinds of vegetables, strawberries and blackberries. What a difference from growing a little bean in a pot! At some distance were cornfields with corn that was taller than me. In the front of the house, attracting bumblebees, were fragrant lilac bushes and huge sunflowers. I was familiar with sunflowers and knew they had seeds that were good to eat.

The family had a large room with dried corn piled to the ceiling. I had fun helping get the kernels off and into a bowl by rubbing two cobs together. This family did not have brooms like we did at home. To sweep the floors, which were clay, they first sprinkled water to keep the dust down and then used thin branches tied together as a broom.

The people in the house treated me well. I loved the smell of fresh bread baking in the clay-floored room, with its large table that had room for everyone to sit at during mealtimes. Besides their grown children, who helped with the farm work, a couple of Soviet soldiers were housed there. These soldiers made me feel safe, not only because they reminded me of the soldiers from the ghetto, but also because they chased away a drunk Soviet soldier who tried to climb through the window, looking for a woman. My bed was full of pillows and it had a thick bedcover, all filled with feathers that were soft and comforting. With no school to go to and lots to eat, I did not miss living in the city. The only thing that made me sad was seeing a man put tiny kittens into a sack to drown them in the river, and the only thing that bothered me was the flies.

In less than a month, Kati and I were taken back to Budapest. My aunt Margaret returned safely from Buchenwald, and the apartment was filled with more adults and children than it could hold. With so many buildings bombed, many people were homeless. Naturally, if an apartment was empty because a Jewish family had been forced to leave it, it was immediately claimed by people who needed a home. Disposing of the furniture and other belongings of the former occupants was also not a problem. Eager neighbours and other looters took care of that. So when Aunt Serena, Uncle Latzi, Aunt Margaret and Uncle Vili returned to Budapest, they ended up with no home and no belongings except for the clothes on their backs.

Jewish organizations from the United States came to the rescue.

They opened up orphanages for the children who had no parents or whose parents had no homes. Kati and I, upon arrival in Budapest, were immediately transported to such an orphanage, while Imre and Hedi were reunited with Aunt Serena, their mother. In this quick move from train to orphanage, nobody told us that while we were in the countryside, my beloved grandmother Franceska had died. All Aunt Margaret said to us was that our stay at the orphanage did not have to be forever, because once she had a place of her own, we would always have a home with her.

~

When Kati and I arrived at the orphanage, we were amazed to see such a beautiful place and a lovely neighbourhood. A wealthy family must have lived there before the war, but now it had been converted into an orphanage to be occupied by Jewish war orphans.

I remember it well. It was a stately two-storey villa with large rooms. The girls slept on the first floor, the boys on the second. There were bunk beds lined up on either side of the room. On the main floor, there was a large dining room with long tables for the hungry bunch. In a corner sat a piano, its black and white keys exposed like a big toothy smile. Whoever wished to play it could, and among us were children who knew how. We stood around that piano and sang the Hebrew songs that we learned there.

I loved being in this orphanage, which was called a Miha – I made friends there and we bonded, playing Ping-Pong and other sports, dancing the hora and singing Hebrew songs. In the girls' room, we whispered about the boys and shared our clothing so we never had to wear the same dress the next day. We had so much fun! It was great to be a child again.

In the evenings, we had meetings and learned about Jewish history. We were taught that Jewish people should be proud because our people had given the world good rules to live by: the Ten Commandments. We were told that at one time our people lived in a land of

Jews called Israel, and now that we were no longer slaves we should again make that place our homeland. We needed to build and defend this land so we would never be unwanted and abused by others again. We were going to be Zionists, the fighters for our freedom, the builders of our homeland. So we learned to set up tents and cook our meals over an open fire. We got stronger by playing endurance games, and learned to fight and defend ourselves by playing games of war. I no longer was scared. I was proud to be a Jew.

Kati: Regaining Our Self-respect

It's little wonder that I was apprehensive and reluctant to enter an orphanage. In my readings about orphanages and other institutions for children, I found out that the people in charge were mean and often abusive. Yet, as usual in my short twelve years of life, I had no choice but to go where I was told.

Except this place, located on a tree-lined boulevard leading to Heroes' Square, beside a large park, was different from what I had imagined. The orphanage was in a most extravagant mansion, never before seen by a child used to rundown, tall apartment buildings in the city and, briefly, the simple country cottage of my recent experience away from Budapest. Inside were lots of large rooms. The first floor had space for couches and armchairs, a large dining room table with chairs all around it and still more empty space. The cooking was done out of sight by hired cooks, I suppose, and the second floor housed many beds in different bedrooms. I was given a bed of my own on the girls' side, and for the first time in a long while, I felt safe.

After a good sleep I got to meet my fellow orphans and the staff. We sat around the table and sang songs – not in Hungarian, but in Hebrew. In fact, everything had a Hebrew name. The children all had Hebrew names as well. I knew that my sister's Hebrew name was Miriam because our mother had told us that when Ilonka was born, a heartbroken man came to the maternity ward of the hospital and

asked if any of the women would name her baby girl after his wife
to honour her memory. My mother felt his pain and let her baby be
named Miriam to give that poor man some comfort. As I said earlier, our family was not religious, although I had seen my mother
light candles on Friday nights and say a blessing over them, but as the
persecution got stronger, this outward show of our respect for God
stopped. So I never learned my Hebrew name, although I suppose
I was given one at birth. Now, at the orphanage, it was up to me to
choose my own Hebrew name.

This orphanage, called a Miha, was wonderful. It provided not
only for our physical needs, but also help in healing our souls, by having what I would now consider counselling and group therapy. The
Miha was run by a Zionist group that believed the atrocities committed against the Jews should never be allowed to happen again, and
the only answer for us was to regain our independence from other
nations, which merely tolerated us and at whose mercy we were. We
needed to have a homeland of our own. We were taught that the Jews
were not pariahs but a proud people who told the world about an al-
mighty invisible God who created everyone equal. We learned to be
proud to be Jews.

In addition to singing songs in Hebrew, we learned to dance the
hora, a Hebrew folk dance. Both boys and girls went out to the large
Heroes' Square to play soccer, which taught us cooperation. We were
never punished, even when some of the rude boys told disgusting
stories at dinner to make the younger kids leave the table to throw
up so they could eat their share, too. We also had group discussions
where we were encouraged to explore and talk about what had happened to us and to our families.

I remember one girl whose name was Lailah. When she looked at
Ilonka, she said that she too had had a sister but now she was dead.
I found out that Lailah and her sister were identical twins, and in
the concentration camp they had been in, the doctors experimented
on twins. They did terrible things to one and kept the other normal

mal so they could compare the results. I was furious with the adults of the world who did such awful things to innocent human beings. I thought, when I grow up, I shall get even and do mean things to others. But as I continued in my learning and my group discussions, although my anger did not subside – it is still with me – I gained the insight that anger should not be directed toward individuals but against injustice, prejudice and greed. So I decided that I would fight those evils, but not by the methods used against the Jews. To signify my commitment, I decided to give myself the Hebrew name Tovah, which in English means "goodness." All the children thirteen and older at the Miha had, as a group, a special Jewish coming-of-age ceremony called a bar (for boys) and bat (for girls) mitzvah in a synagogue. I was called to the Torah by my new Hebrew name, Tovah, and I was proud.

~

The world did not stand still while we were healing our souls. Both my aunt Margaret and uncle Vili survived the war. Uncle Vili was now crippled because his leg had been injured in a concentration camp, and my aunt Margaret carried a terrible secret, which she kept from her sister Gizi, about her daughter, my cousin Magda, who never came back from Buchenwald. My aunt Margaret found her niece Magda when they were both were assigned to a labour group that went out to the fields to collect crops and do other backbreaking chores. Such work did have an advantage: in the fields were edible crops, and although they were raw, Aunt Margaret and the others were able to eat some secretly. One day, my cousin Magda refused to go and stayed behind, hiding in a bunk bed. When the women came back, they found Magda's body: she had been tortured and beaten to death. She had just turned seventeen. Auntie Gizi never learned how her only child met her death, not from her sister, nor from me.

Aunt Margaret, my role model, was a fighter. Once back in Hungary, she not only got back her means for making a good living by selling poultry in her stall at the open market, she also did the impossible: she found a big apartment, which she actually doubled in size. She did this by offering to rebuild, at her own expense, the bombed-out apartment next to the one she was granted by the now-Communist government. With a double-sized apartment, she had room enough for her sons and her sister Gizi, who was now alone, since neither her daughter nor her husband had returned.

Aunt Margaret and Uncle Vili were among the lucky ones whose whole family survived the Holocaust. Their son Tibi, once he saw that his parents and brother, Rudi, had survived, decided to take advantage of the confusion that followed the liberation of Hungary and left the country again, forever this time, on his own terms, and went to seek his fortune in South America.

Next, my aunt Serena came home and later, my uncle Latzi. They were reunited with Hedi and Imre, but not with baby Gyurika. Because I was in the Zionist orphanage, I did not know that my two young cousins had also been placed in an orphanage, since my poor aunt Serena was obsessed with finding her youngest child. I heard later from my uncle Latzi that she went all over Hungary trying to find her baby. So even though Hedi and Imre had their mother and father, they were really without their parents for two more years. My uncle confessed to me when I was grown and he was living in Canada with his second wife that to stop Serena's fruitless and destructive search for Gyurika, he lied to her and said he had proof that their little boy did not survive. This deception stopped Serena from searching further and got their two other children back with them from the orphanage, but they continued to be unhappy. I am sure that somewhere in Hungary there is a grown man with blond hair and blue eyes who thinks he knows who his mother is and will never find out that he had another mother, who loved him very much.

Our dear German auntie, Helen, was now free to marry her Hungarian sweetheart, who had been forbidden to her during the Nazi regime because of her Jewish father. With my grandmother dead and my grandfather now blind, Helen lived in the tiny home of Uncle Latzi and Aunt Serena with Hedi and Imre. What became of my poor unprotected Romanian grandma, Mutter, I shall never know.

Ilonka and I waited in vain for our mother's return. Although Aunt Serena knew her fate, she decided never to tell us. I did not find out until forty years later how my mother died, when Ilonka and I visited Hungary with my husband and two of our daughters and paid our respects to Aunt Serena. She finally told me that after the inhabitants were collected from the segregated house where she and our mother lived together, they ended up at Dachau concentration camp after a long and painfully cold march from Hungary. My mother was despondent and extremely worried about our fate. When a wagon came out of Dachau, it was announced that those who were sick or tired could get a ride on it. Aunt Serena told me that she said to my mother, "Borishka, don't get on that wagon – it is a trick." But my mother said she did not care, there was nothing for her to live for anymore, and she climbed onto the wagon.

When I first heard this, I was so angry. Why didn't she fight to stay alive? Why did she give up all hope? Had she not done that, Ilonka and I would not have had to live the rest of our lives as orphans, and she could have experienced the joy of seeing her beautiful grandchildren. I now understand more about depression, and I no longer feel anger but great compassion for this sweet, romantic and loving mother of mine. In spite of everything, after the war was over, Ilonka and I believed that we were not really orphans. We still hoped that our father, who knew many languages and was smart and charming, would have found a way to save himself, and if Aunt Serena, Aunt Margaret and all the others had survived, surely our mother too would come home one day.

~

In all my life up until that time, I was happiest at the Miha. Nobody picked on us, and we children felt a bond not only because of the tragedies in our past but also because of the great plans for our future in a land where we would never be unwelcome guests. And yet, in spite of feeling safe and belonging to a group, getting a chance to play and have fun, I still was not truly happy. The more we learned from our war games how to attack and how to defend ourselves against attackers, the more we sang songs on how we would plant seeds and make a now barren land green again, the more I grew apprehensive about a future in another land where I might have to kill people, and where I would live and work in the country, farming the fields. I loved the kids in my group and I agreed that we should not stay in a country that had betrayed our families and been eager to destroy us. But I could not bear the idea of being in violent confrontation with other people. I thought that I should do only good deeds and never harm anyone. I also did not cherish the prospect of being a farmer, given my dismal experience with the cow in the field. I felt like a traitor when I sang those patriotic songs, knowing that I did not want to live in Israel. How could I sing, eat and play with my friends, even look them in the eye, feeling this way?

I remembered my aunt Margaret's promise that she would always have a place for me in her home. I decided that moving back in with her would solve my dilemma, and I walked to the open market to ask her. I remember that day so well. Now all nicely fattened up, she was standing in the stall, her clothes covered with a greasy white apron. My aunt Gizi and my uncle Vili were standing beside her as I said that I wanted to come and stay with them in their apartment. Aunt Gizi looked at me and asked coldly, "Why? What's the matter where you live?" Until then, it had not occured to me that I might not be welcome. But those few rejecting words were like a knife to my heart and I have never forgotten them, even after many, many years. However, the apartment belonged to Aunt Margaret, and she firmly replied that there was no problem leaving the orphanage, because Ilonka and I were her sister's children, and there would always be room in her home for us. And so, at the age of thirteen, I made what I thought was a life decision: to remain in Hungary and live in Aunt Margaret's home with her family and Aunt Gizi.

The apartment was amazing and it had just about everything anyone could wish for. When you entered from the courtyard, on the left side of the hall was a spacious kitchen with a pantry in the back of it. Next to the kitchen was a small room that was originally the maid's bedroom. Off the hall there was also a small powder room. As the hall turned the corner to the right, there were several entrances into larger rooms. The room at the end of the hall would be for Ilonka and me. Aunt Gizi had the largest room because she had brought her baby grand piano with her. This room had a balcony as well. The next room belonged to Aunt Margaret and Uncle Vili. This particular apartment had been built for the owner of the building, who had made sure it had a bathroom the size of a small room, with a giant sunken bathtub. What a far cry from our little wooden washtub in the kitchen of our tenement apartment. In addition to all the space, Aunt Margaret had had an opening made into an adjoining apartment she paid to rebuild, so that her son Rudi could also live there, later with his future wife.

As the summer of 1945 came to an end and I was no longer part of the Miha, I did not forget the history lessons I had learned there. During the previous year and a half I had missed some of Grade 5 and all of Grade 6. Now I was placed in Grade 7 in an all-girls' school. Most of the students knew each other from before, since this school was in their neighbourhood. We no longer had religious studies as a subject, because Hungary was now under Communist rule. But the system itself had not changed much. We had to show respect for our teachers by standing up when they entered the classroom, and we had to address them formally. They in turn addressed us formally by our last names. After living in the rowdy, egalitarian atmosphere of the Miha, I found the school cold, impersonal and, with the exception of my art teacher, indifferent. None of my fellow students bothered to include me in their groups, and I immediately felt like an outsider. I was not aware of it, but I was rejecting them as well and did not even try to be part of any group. Still, I gained quite a bit of attention from the teachers and my fellow students, because every time the teacher asked a question in class, I was the one with my hand up first, and usually my answers were right. Not that this kind of behaviour made me any more popular among my classmates. However, being able to show off my knowledge gave me quite a bit of smug satisfaction.

I still remembered how hurt I felt when told that I did not belong because I was not a true Hungarian. Well, I decided to agree with them that I did not belong, nor did I want to. I was fourteen and I felt very angry and resentful, not only for the suffering inflicted on my family and me, and for my present situation as an orphan living with relatives, but even more so for the silence, ignorance and lack of caring from my fellow students. I resolved, without getting into any physical altercations using my hand-to-hand combat skills newly acquired at the Miha, to show them all and beat them with knowledge. I had a considerable advantage over my classmates: partly because I was almost two years older than them, but also because during the time I was not allowed to go to school, I had acquired quite a lot of information through my extensive reading of books that were advanced, probably not appropriate for a child, and certainly beyond the experience of most girls my age. With my mind made up that I would prove to my teachers and my classmates that I was not the bad person they assumed a Jewish girl to be, but in fact I was much better, I proceeded to compete with my classmates in all subjects.

In Grades 7 and 8 at that time there was a terrible system of comparing child to child on the report cards. Every student received a number from one to five in each subject, and this determined her standing in her studies. The number was written on the report card for everyone to see. I wanted to stand first, with everyone below me. By the end of the first term, I had achieved my aim. I do not feel proud of my fourteen-year-old self, because in my eagerness to win – and just like the people who had devised the system – I never thought of the feelings of those whose academic standing did not measure up to the expected level. I am happy to say that later, as a more mature adult, I made amends: I became a teacher for children with special needs, and over the years helped many of them succeed at school.

The only time in class that I relaxed from competing with my schoolmates was during art lessons, perhaps because in art there are no right or wrong answers. We had a soft-spoken gentle teacher, who actually talked to me and said that she thought I showed some talent. She even invited me to her and her husband's home on the beautiful mountainous Buda side of the city, and offered me individual lessons free, provided my family allowed me to come. I went gladly, without bothering to ask permission from Aunt Margaret. At the age of fourteen, I lived my life quite independently. School started at eight in the morning and finished by one o'clock. I had a student pass for transportation, so in the afternoons I could go wherever I pleased, since the only adult who cared was Aunt Margaret. She worked at the market until closing, and by the time she got home she was too tired to chat or ask me any questions. Besides, being in charge of myself since the ghetto, I was quite used to wandering around and exploring on my own.

Staying in the apartment did offer Ilonka and me safety, food and shelter, but I didn't find much pleasure in being there. Uncle Vili was a nice man who loved to cook and eat. That is all I knew of him, since he said very little of any significance, if anything at all. Although he was twelve years Aunt Margaret's senior, he followed Aunt Margaret's decisions, including taking us into his home – I am sure at some inconvenience. Unlike my sister, who watched and admired every move of Uncle Vili's in the kitchen and learned to be a very good cook herself, I paid attention to food only when it was ready to eat, so I did not have much interest in his activities.

Aunt Gizi never got over the loss of her sweet husband and her beloved daughter, Magda. She just existed. At times, she worked with Margaret and Vili at the market; in general she isolated herself at home from Ilonka and me. During the two years we lived under the same roof, she never once thought of giving us lessons on the piano that sat silently in the corner of her room, nor would she let me read any of the books she kept locked up in a large cabinet. The irony was, here was a mother without the child she loved, and here were her own sister's two love-hungry youngsters who needed, and would so much have appreciated, even a small amount of love from their aunt. But she had nothing to give. Her heart was locked up from us, just like the books in the cabinet and the keys on the piano.

Still, I was quite happy to keep my distance from Aunt Gizi. I remembered well how, a lifetime ago, she would smack my fingers if I made a mistake at the piano. Nor did I forget how she had tolerated my mother as a poor relation. But most of all, I knew that she resented our very existence because her own child was gone. Aunt Gizi's rejection hurts even now, but I should like to add that when I grew up and had my own home in Canada, I showed more compassion for this sad, bitter lady in her old age than she did for me when I was a child, and I honoured my mother's memory by welcoming Gizi to my home and making her feel accepted.

The person who created misery for me at Aunt Margaret's place was her son, my cousin Rudi. It may be true that people don't change their basic nature from childhood to old age. Having survived slave labour and Soviet captivity, Rudi thrived in his new-found freedom. He was a good-looking, well-built young man, and was liked by many girls for his charm, funny jokes and handsomeness. When Rudi was not out chasing girls, or perhaps even looking for work, he amused himself by trying to torment me. He knew that I loved to read, so he found the books I borrowed from the library and hid them. The more I showed my frustration, the happier Rudi got. When I finally told on him to Aunt Margaret, she slapped him across the face and ordered him never to do anything to hurt her sister's child, or he would have to answer to her.

Well, he left me alone pretty much after that, until the end of the school year, when I got my Grade 7 report card with my standing in the class: first. Uncle Latzi bought me a used bicycle as a gift for being such a good student. I was excited about it until the next morning, when I discovered Rudi had taken my precious bike and given it to his fiancée without even talking to me first. I decided not to complain to Aunt Margaret. There was not much point in it, since Rudi was her son, and she and Uncle Vili were busy preparing for his wedding.

Since I could not do much at home to avoid Rudi, during the last part of Grade 7, I spent the afternoons not only wandering around my neighbourhood, but also exploring the city. I heard about a place where you could get special treats like canned fruit and chocolates if you were Jewish. This magical place was in an office building in the heart of Budapest and it was called the "Joint." When I went in and told the staff that my parents had not come back after the war, I was received as a most welcome lost child. They showered me with canned peaches and pineapple, along with lots of Hershey chocolate bars, and told me to come back soon. I went home carrying these gifts, eating my share of chocolates on the way and saving enough to give Ilonka.

The Joint, I now know, refers to the American Jewish Joint Distribution Committee, a worldwide Jewish relief organization. Set up in 1914 to assist Jews affected by World War I, after the Holocaust it provided assistance to the remaining Jewish communities of Europe. I suppose it was the same idea as the welfare programs of our cities in Canada, but unlike those programs, its ways and spirit were far different. At the Joint I did not need to prove that I was needy, nor did people there show that they were sorry for me. They actually made me feel that I was doing them a favour by visiting and accepting their gifts. Of course, I was not aware that I really *was* special in their eyes because a million and a half children had been murdered in the Holocaust, and I represented a small fraction of those who had survived.

At the Joint I was like a member of the family, and everybody was like an aunt or uncle. So when my art teacher told me that I was now past the stage where she could teach me and I should go to a professional program for adults, I just walked into the director's office and told him that I needed money to get into an art program. He asked me if I could show him my work. I said that I did not have anything with me, but if he handed me a piece of paper and a pen or pencil, I would show him how I could draw. This white-haired gentleman sat quietly at his desk while I drew a quick portrait of him. I gave him the portrait, and he authorized payment to a studio for my lessons.

At the studio there were several easels and chairs placed around an elevated area for the model. The main artist and proprietor of the studio provided all the materials and hired the models who posed nude for us. As far as I remember, except for the model, I was the only female there, and the only child. The models were mostly women, although sometimes a man would pose as well. We had only a short period for sketching each pose to get the essence of the subject. The person in charge rarely needed to guide me, and said that by the end of the summer I should be ready for a show. I was so proud of myself! I told Aunt Margaret that now I would have a chance to get started on a serious career as an artist. Aunt Margaret became upset and promptly forbade me ever to go to the studio again. She said it did not matter if I was talented. Only a few artists made a living from their art; all the others starved. It would be much better for me when I finished Grade 8 if I joined her at the market and learned to become a businesswoman.

I was devastated. I wrote in my diary, begging my mother to come to my aid, but there was no answer. My total helplessness apparently showed itself through a reaction in my body, because both hands broke out in a horrible rash. The rest of me seemed to be fine, so to keep busy and feel accepted, I kept going to see the friendly staff at the Joint. There, I found a way to escape from all my sorrows. They told me that if I wanted, I could leave Hungary and be adopted by a family in another country, and my sister could, too. This offer was part of a program sponsored worldwide by Jewish organizations that sought to find and help the children who had survived. Jews in many countries were asked to, or offered to, take in these orphans and bring them up as their own children.

This opportunity appeared to answer my prayer to my mother for help. I would not have to live among people who did not accept me and whose polite indifference I did not trust. I would not have to avoid my cousin Rudi at home. And I would not have to chop up dead chickens and geese to sell after I finished Grade 8! I could have a chance to become an artist in a faraway country where no one would ever call me a "dirty Jew." I told the staff at the Joint that I wanted to leave. They said I had a choice: I could go to Australia, South Africa or Canada.

I decided on Canada. My decision was based on knowing that both South Africa and Australia had strong racial policies regarding their black and aboriginal populations. I thought that was wrong. Discrimination against anyone was still discrimination, and I didn't want to be any place where such a thing still happened. My knowledge of Canada was quite limited, since my interest in reading did not include social geography. I knew that Canada was a very large country, it was very cold, hardly any people lived in it and they spoke English. It seemed to me the perfect place to get away from everyone.

Although I thought I was completely in charge of my own life, in reality this was not so. Unbeknownst to me, Aunt Margaret was now the legal guardian for Ilonka and me, and she was the one to make such decisions for us. My aunt loved her sister's daughters as if they were her own. Much later, she told me how she was torn about letting us leave her care, especially while we were so young. She wrote to her son Tibi in Argentina about her dilemma. My cousin, who was the first in the family to leave Hungary, replied that she had no right to keep us away from a better future. Because of her son's advice, Aunt Margaret gave the Joint her consent for us to leave her home and be adopted by a family in Canada.

My sister had not really planned to go anywhere. Although she missed the friends she had made at the orphanage, she loved being in the dance and gymnastics classes that Aunt Margaret had enrolled her in, and unlike me, she got along well with everyone at home, including Aunt Gizi. The only reason Ilonka was willing to leave this loving home for a strange and distant place was the same reason she had left the Miha: she did not want to be separated from me.

Ilonka: Into the Unknown

Although I missed the excitement and friendship of the Miha, living at Aunt Margaret's place in a real home was fine. The apartment was already occupied by her family members when Kati and I moved in. There was Uncle Vili, Aunt Margaret's husband, who had been shot by the Nazis and could not work in the open market during the cold winters. He had lots of arthritic pain, walked slowly with a cane and often could not sleep. He told me that when he was in a concentration camp, I don't know which one, they made him dig his own grave and then they shot him into it. He just pretended he was dead. Once it was dark, he crawled out from the grave and managed to hide in the forest. He was able to survive there until the Americans liberated that part of Germany. He never complained about his pain, but helped out in the market during the warm weather and cooked the most delicious meals for the family.

I enjoyed being with Uncle Vili, sitting with him in the warm kitchen. I loved watching this bald little man with the big belly chop and stir, loved smelling the aromas that came out of those pots. He created dishes fit for a king's palate, not to mention his own. Uncle Vili enjoyed his own cooking, as we all did, and his well-rounded body showed it. Always hungry, I listened to him explain important details as he cooked. My reward, in addition to the learning and entertainment, was that I had the chance to be the first to taste his creations. I admired his talents, and in turn, I think he enjoyed my company and admiration.

Uncle Vili was a kind gentleman. He looked quite elegant as he strolled to a neighbourhood coffee house where he met his friends to talk about the good old days and the politics of the world. Aunt Margaret and Uncle Vili were a loving couple. I never heard any arguments between them like I used to hear between my parents. Actually, whatever Aunt Margaret said was just fine with him. Because Aunt Margaret owned the poultry business, she was the one who provided for everyone in her family, which included not only Uncle Vili but also their son Rudi, Aunt Gizi, Kati and me.

My cousin Rudi lived in the apartment too, and after he married, so did his wife, Magda, who was one of the fortunate young women who survived the horrors of the camps. Rudi and Magda were about twenty years old. Magda knew about makeup and hairstyles. I think she studied to be a beautician, while Rudi learned to be a furrier like our uncle Latzi. I am not sure that at that stage of their careers they were able to support themselves financially, especially since Hungary was just recovering from a war that it had lost.

Our aunt Gizi moved in with Uncle Vili and Aunt Margaret because she had lost her own apartment when she was forced to live in the Budapest ghetto; once a Jewish family's apartment was vacated, it was immediately assigned to a family who was not Jewish. Since Aunt Gizi's husband and daughter never came back from the camps, she clung to her sister, Margaret, for support and love, just as I clung to mine. She helped Aunt Margaret at the stall in the open market, although she was never very good at selling. In reality, Aunt Margaret shouldered the financial responsibility for looking after us all.

Aunt Margaret never acted as though she minded all the work she did. She told me that she had always wanted a daughter, and she was glad that she had Kati and me to fuss over. She bought a huge phosphorous-orange parachute on the black market, and paid a dressmaker to sew dresses for Kati and me. Whenever we went out in the street in our glowing orange dresses, people could see us from far away. They would say, "Here come the Mozes sisters!" We were both embarrassed, but at that time not much else was available to wear. She tried to comfort us by saying, "But it is real silk!" That did not help.

I had to go back to school – into Grade 5 – after missing about two years. The other girls had learned arithmetic, but nobody had taught me. I did not want to tell anyone that I could not do subtraction, multiplication or division. I just felt stupid and tried to stay in the back of the classroom so I would not be questioned. I was miserable at school; not only had I fallen behind in arithmetic, but Aunt Margaret had put me not into a regular school but a nearby Jewish school. I think she did this to protect me from kids who might still pick on me for being Jewish. I was aware, by then, that even though the Hungarians had lost the war, it didn't change the way they thought. Many of them still thought – and decades later some still do – that everything bad that happened to them was the fault of the Jews. I did not want to be picked on ever again, because I knew I had not done anything bad.

My new problem was that my classmates were religious, and the teachers made us pray every day in Hebrew and memorize these prayers. I did not know what I was saying. They did translate the prayers for us into Hungarian so we would know the meaning, but once we learned one Hebrew prayer they taught us another, then another and another, each with a different meaning, and I forgot the meaning of the ones that came before. This school was confusing. It just overloaded my brain with things that did not make much sense to me, and I didn't like going to school at all.

But at Aunt Margaret's home I was loved and happy. Aunt Margaret, an angel in disguise, signed me up for tap, ballet and acrobatics in a special dance school. I loved it! I practised every day and looked forward to the weekly class when I could participate. I ruined many of my skirts by cutting them short and lopsided to make dance outfits. Aunt Margaret overlooked my wasting the money she spent on my clothes. I showed my gratitude by styling her hair, combing and brushing it while she sat patiently and endured my fussing over her. This dear aunt never criticized or put us down, and she never got mad at me for anything. She was also generous as well as caring, giving Kati and me money for movies and treats, and she made sure that we had warm clothes and good shoes. Of all the grown-ups, next to my mother she loved me best. I wonder how my life would have turned out if I had stayed in her home until I was grown.

Unfortunately, Kati did not want to stay. She had heard there were people in Canada who wanted to adopt children, support them and pay for their education just like real parents. With tears in her eyes, Aunt Margaret gave her permission and let us go, thinking that it would be in our best interests for a better future. My sister wanted to take a chance, and although I suppose that, at eleven, I could have said that I wanted to stay, I did not wish to be apart from Kati. I loved my aunt and uncle, and I did not want to leave them, but I did not want to leave my sister either.

I don't believe I would have ever wanted to leave Aunt Margaret and Uncle Vili's home, where I felt loved and safe, if Kati had not wanted to leave Hungary forever to go to Canada. Just like in the Miha, I could not see myself living without Kati, so I told my aunt and uncle that I wanted to go to Canada, too.

It took a whole year of waiting while doctors examined Kati and me and officials filled out all sorts of formal documents and sent them back and forth between the two countries. Finally, in the summer of 1948, we got the visas that allowed us to leave Hungary and be admitted to Canada. Kati and I looked forward to this trip as a big adventure. We could hardly wait to go by train to Paris, then by boat to London, then to board a ship, a real ocean liner. It was so exciting!

At last the day arrived. I said goodbye to my friends, helped my aunt put my clothes into a suitcase and tied it with a rope. On the way to the train station, Aunt Margaret held my hand tightly and gave me a small bag of candy to sweeten the parting, while Aunt Gizi told Kati several times to take good care of me. At last we climbed the steps into the train and each grabbed a seat by the window before anyone else could. Leaning out, we waved our final goodbyes. The whistle blew and slowly the train moved forward, leaving the Nyugati Railway Station for the unknown.

Kati: Not So Fast

Once it was decided that Ilonka and I would leave Hungary and go to Canada to be adopted, I was ready to leave immediately. But Canada took its time processing our papers, and as the months dragged on, I had to go to school. I now attended Grade 8 in body, but I no longer cared to prove anything by standing first. Most of the time I went to my classes, but every so often, when the weather was good, I skipped them and went around the city all by myself, imagining I was a tourist who was seeing beautiful Budapest for the first – and probably the last – time. I tried to etch the sights in my mind so I would remember them when I was far away.

Surprisingly, I did not lose much of my standing at school. I just slipped to second place from first. Nobody noticed or cared, either. I graduated from Grade 8 without much fanfare, in spite of the fact that Grade 8 was the final year at that school. One might have thought that the school and the parents would have a party for the graduates. I do not recall any such celebration, perhaps because there was nothing much to celebrate.

The upper classes of Hungarian society had a special program of education that continued well after the eighth grade, called a *gimnázium*, which would be similar to high school in Canada. This program included such subjects as physics, chemistry, mathematics, literature and languages, including Latin, to those children who would later become the nation's doctors, lawyers and political leaders. Such an education cost a lot of money and was not funded by the state. The children of the working-class poor of Hungary went to my kind of school, which was called *polgári,* meaning "for the public." It did not cost parents anything and going there did not lead anywhere. We learned just enough mathematics to get by in general financial transactions at stores, and we memorized poetry.

Most of the girls at my school planned to stay at home once they were married, and the boys from the program would continue their training as apprentices in various trades. There was no such thing as a guidance department to advise the family of a talented boy to plan for the future, other than entering the work force as a tradesman, or in the case of a girl, preparing for marriage by training to be a good cook, housekeeper and, most important, obedient wife.

We learned a song in our music class, which in translation said:

To bake to cook to sew
You really have to know
For if in these you don't succeed
The school of life will fail you.

I never did learn any of those skills very well, not even after I got married and had children.

~

It was eleven o'clock in the morning on an August day in 1948 when Aunt Margaret closed up my suitcase and Ilonka's in the hallway. Aunt Gizi, eyes all red, kept saying, "Take good care of yourselves and behave respectably. Kati, don't go out in the street without a scarf, and make sure that your sister also dresses warmly in Canada." Aunt Margaret kept hugging us, and after that we put on our coats, even though it was summertime, because in Canada it would be cold. She then put a small parcel of food into our hands so we'd have something to eat on the train.

There was already a group of young people at the station, as well as a lady named Mrs. Pape, who was to accompany us to Paris. As soon as our aunts saw her, they started to ask: "What can be expected for the children?" "How long will the trip take?" "When will the children leave Paris?" "Where will they get on the ship?" "Who will adopt the children?" and many more similar questions. They did not get any answers, since Mrs. Pape had no real information about anything, just like the bigger kids I asked.

Aunt Margaret's eyes were watery, even though she kept a smile on her face. She kept talking about all sorts of comical things in a weird sort of way, yet the whole time, her talk did not feel funny to me, just sad. Finally, the porter picked up our luggage and we had to get into the train. Just before we climbed the steps, she told me once more, "Take care of the little one." I promised her that she need not worry. Indeed, I took those words into my heart, and they have guided me throughout my life, not only in looking after my sister but later, when I became an adult, in looking after other children in need as well.

As the train whistled, we left Budapest and kept waving with smiling faces to people along the way until we reached Újpest. The train sped up, and to me it seemed to be flying. I observed that in our group of children, there were some kids who looked quite grown up. We arrived that evening at the Austrian-Hungarian border, but nobody examined our luggage. The train stood for two hours in Vienna while other people's bags were checked. Unfortunately, we had no chance to get off the train to see anything of Vienna, but I did hear some people make comments about us in German, which I understood. They said that while their children were starving, we were still alive. I was happy when we finally left that station to continue on to Switzerland. As we travelled through that country of mountains, waterfalls and green pastures toward France, I wrote a note in my diary that those people were the reason I had lost my parents and had to leave my home to go to a strange place far away from everything that I had ever known.

In Paris we were taken to a lovely villa in a suburb of the city. The mansion, with its many spacious rooms, reminded me of the Miha in Budapest, but it also had a fairly large area of land around it. We met quite a few young people who were also staying there temporarily. They, just like us, were children who had survived the Holocaust, except they did not speak Hungarian, since they were from other countries. I remember a young girl, about fourteen years old, who said she was from Belgium, while some others were from Poland and some from France as well. Most of these boys and girls were destined for South Africa and Australia, and like us were being housed in the villa while they waited for officials at their various destinations to finalize their permit papers to enter the country. In the meantime, all any of us could do was wait. I was bored for weeks and weeks, with nothing to do, nothing to read and nowhere to go.

Those who could speak French went out to movies and on sight-seeing trips into Paris. I wanted very much to go with them, as I had read quite a few accounts of the wonders of that glittering city, but I did not speak French well and I didn't trust the opportunistic boys who offered to be our guides. Most of them were a couple of years older than I was, and some were even older than their officially declared age of just under eighteen. Some were a bit too friendly with the young girls, who loved the attention they received from them. I remember talking to a sixteen-year-old Hungarian girl who had developed a crush on a handsome street-smart boy named Karl. They kissed a lot, and Karl was coaxing the girl to do even more than that. At the wise old age of fifteen, I advised her that she should do no such thing, because no matter what, the girl always ended up paying the price. Karl would be long gone to South Africa, while she would be left crying. I have no idea if the girl listened to my advice, but I watched my sister like a hawk, since, like my mother, she was quite a romantic.

After about three long weeks, our papers arrived and along with a group of Hungarian- and French-speaking young people, we were taken across the English Channel to London, where we were to stay in a public shelter overnight before being transported to Southampton to sail across the Atlantic. That day we saw nothing of London except for the building we were housed in for the night.

In France we had been given tasty and interesting meals that were quite different from the Hungarian cuisine of my uncle Vili's, but England had nothing to offer in this respect. For dinner we were taken into a sparsely furnished dining area with long bare tables set with plates and cutlery. My plate had a large slice of baloney covering it, and some sad vegetables on the side. I was hungry, and with my knife and fork I proceeded to cut a piece of the meat. As soon as I put my fork into the baloney, the fork hit the plate with a clink. That baloney was so thin it was more like a painted illusion than a real slice of meat. Having come from Aunt Margaret's home, where we had an amazing amount of food that my aunt and uncle brought home from the open market, this meagre meal was quite a shock to me. When I asked for a second helping, I was told that everyone in London had only what food the ration tickets supplied. This is how I found out that even though the British had won the war three years earlier, they were still quite poor. England never seemed terribly attractive to me again. I was now looking forward to leaving it the next morning to get on an ocean liner and head for new adventures in Canada.

Ilonka: New Priorities

What an adventure, sailing with Kati on this huge ship called the *Aquitania*, across the Atlantic Ocean! I had never seen such a large body of water, nor had I ever seen a ship before except in picture books. At thirteen years of age, I had a long life of many more wonders and discoveries ahead of me. Just like the other orphans in our group, I had high expectations – because of the promises that people at the Joint had made – of what life would be like once I was adopted and living in my new home.

My number one priority at that age was to find substitute parents, since I very much missed my mother and father, who had doted on me because I was the baby. In their eyes, I could do no wrong, and I was admired and praised for whatever I did. Kati tried to act as a substitute parent, but it was not the same; she just told me what to do and not do. I knew she cared, but she was too bossy. I tried to listen and do as she told me, but sometimes, when she wasn't around, I didn't.

Food was priority number two. Even though I was not really hungry, I somehow thought that I might soon feel starved. Just like some of the other kids with whom I was travelling, I worried that sooner or later the ship's hospitality would stop. So after we finished our daily meal, we would hoard what we didn't eat under our shirts or in our pockets to take back to our cabin, in case food was not given to us the next day. In the cabin, I would hide the smuggled food under my pillow.

My third priority was to have friends. Although I fell seasick a few times when the ocean got stormy and menacing, and that forced me to stay in our crowded cabin, the rough weather did not last long in August. Once the ship felt steady again I bravely emerged from below and walked on the huge deck among the passengers, a little pale but unafraid. I became friends with a young English boy, and we found each other fascinating. Even though we could not understand each other's languages, there was an attraction. We strolled together on the deck, looked at the never-ending ocean and held hands when nobody was around. He taught me my first English song. It did not matter that I did not know what it meant. It went like this:

One-sy, two-sy, I love you-sy,
Three-sy, four-sy, you love me-sy,
Five-sy, six-sy, start again-sy,
One-sy, two-sy, I love you-sy.

We sang it every evening as we walked together on the deck, holding hands. Ah, puppy love! Once the *Aquitania* docked in the port of Halifax, we never saw each other again, but I never forgot him.

Kati: Arrival to a New Life

The air in Halifax on August 23, 1948, was extremely hot and humid, not at all like what I had expected from my readings about the Land of Ice and Snow. That should have given me a clue that life in Canada for Ilonka and me might not turn out to be all that we had been led to believe.

Our group was met by a lady who I thought would accompany us to our various destinations. I was struck by her unnatural appearance. She was slim, like a young person my age, with shiny, youthful-looking hair, but her face was sunken and full of wrinkles. In spite of her effort to appear young by putting on rouge and lipstick and wearing pretty clothes, to me she still looked like a shrivelled-up old woman, just the opposite of my beautiful, roly-poly aunt Margaret. I believe she was there to make sure that we had all our landing papers properly filled out, processed and stamped, and that we would all be put safely on the train that was to go across Canada to all its major cities.

So again, we were on a train, travelling toward unknown places and new experiences. Our lengthy trip on this train taught me that I was not wrong about Canada being enormous. As the train sped across the land for hours and hours and the day turned into night, I could tell that we were still in the middle of nowhere, with nothing in sight when I looked out the window but unpopulated fields. Once it got dark, the porters pulled down some beds from the ceiling for us to sleep in, and when we woke up in the morning, we were still travelling. By now, we could have crossed all of Europe! Finally, the train stopped in Montreal, and all those who spoke French got off. The rest of us stayed on and continued to Toronto, after which the train was bound for Winnipeg and Vancouver.

In Toronto we were met by yet another lady, who took us to a large house in the middle of the city, on the corner of Harbord and Markham streets. It was the property of the Jewish community and at times had been used as a Jewish library, but now it was housing the newly arrived survivors of the Holocaust. I learned from some Hungarian-speaking young people that, just like those who were already housed here, we would be staying in this residence temporarily, only until our social workers found us a place to live. I noticed that there was only one child, a boy younger than Ilonka, and he had an older brother and sister along with him. I also noticed, with some concern, that while we were treated very well by the adults who prepared our meals, nobody talked about adopting any of us.

After a few days at this reception centre, our English education started. Our group was walked to a nearby school, where a pleasant-looking teacher gave us some picture books and proceeded to teach us some simple but important verb forms in the language. I parroted them – "I am, you are, he is, she is, we are, you are, they are"– and eagerly copied down everything in sight. Then, in the wisdom of the Jewish Family and Child Service, after this crash course in English, a social worker came for my sister but not for me. We were told that Ilonka – whom the social worker now called Ellen – would be placed in a permanent home with a family and would be their daughter. So after all those terrible years when I so fiercely protected her and she clung to me for love and security, those "wise" social workers separated us, leaving us each to manage on our own in a strange environment.

To reassure me, I was shown her new home in a two-storey, three-bedroom house near Bathurst Street and Ava Road, in a very clean neighbourhood. There I was introduced to a woman, a man and their two sons, one of them about my age and the other a bit younger. I was assured that I could visit Ellen any time I wanted. Although I had never thought that we would be apart, I felt sure that my sister would be well cared for by this nice family. And so she was – for a little while.

~

It seems that the Joint's staff members in Hungary were unaware of what would happen to the orphans in the various countries they were sent to. I am sure that the Joint officials, who were caring and sincere, did not mislead my mother's sister on purpose. However, they had no idea that the prospective adoptive parents in other countries were under the misconception that the children who had survived the Holocaust would be adoptable babies and young children. People in Canada, even after the horrific conditions during the Nazi persecutions became known, did not quite comprehend that most young children could not have survived without a parent, unless they were hidden. A small chance of survival was more likely for older children, who could possibly fend for themselves without adults. Thus, the children who survived and came to Canada were not lovable little boys and girls but troubled youngsters with memories of their lost families as well as of the circumstances surrounding their survival. Three years had passed since the end of the war, and having lived as orphans since then, they were now entering their teenage years. This stage of life is turbulent for most adolescents, let alone those who had experiences as traumatic as the ones of some of the people in my group.

Not surprisingly, not many families in Toronto were ready to adopt a distrustful, independent and rebellious teenager who could not even speak English. Many of the orphans were not at all concerned about being adopted. Most – as old as seventeen, even older

– were happy just to be supported while they got a chance at free education that would enable them to make a living. Indeed, after being on their own for years, many preferred to live independently without close supervision by adults who would tell them what to do. At the ages of fifteen and thirteen, my sister and I were not among them. In spite of thinking that I was a capable, independent person, I had never truly been on my own. I, who was more curious than rebellious, and my sister, who loved to be with people and was eager to please, wished very much to be part of a family and to have parents again, just as was promised to us and to Aunt Margaret.

The social worker assigned to my case was named Miss Spivak. She was a pretty young woman with a wide smile, and based on how she saw to the needs of a fifteen-year-old girl who knew nothing about the ways of the city and couldn't even speak the language, I now think she had probably just graduated from a school of social work. Her job was to find a place for me to live. Miss Spivak showed me several rooms for rent, and I came to understand that she was trying to get me to be a tenant in one of these places, with the understanding that the Jewish Family and Child Service would be responsible for the rent while I attended school. There would be no family for me, just a rented room. I strongly objected to this arrangement, and I said no to each place. I do not remember how I communicated this to Miss Spivak, but I finally got her to understand that my aunt let my sister and me come to Canada only because the Joint's people in Hungary had promised her – and Ilonka and me as well – that we would not be on our own but part of a family. The next time Miss Spivak came to see me at the reception centre, she informed me that she had found a family for me.

When I first arrived in Toronto, I was impressed by how different it appeared from Budapest. Having come from a heavily populated part of Budapest, where people generally lived in large apartment buildings and green vegetation was confined to parks, I was amazed to see, on all the streets, row after row of small houses, each with a front yard and backyard that had green grass and bushes and flowers growing. Toronto seemed like an overgrown version of the village that I stayed in for a short while after the war in Hungary, even though I knew that it was a large city with thousands and thousands of people.

My new family lived on the first floor of one of those small houses, while the second floor was occupied by my foster mother's brother and his family. Although this was not an apartment but a house, the living space was actually much smaller than that of Aunt Margaret's luxury apartment. The living and dining rooms, kitchen and two bedrooms were all half the size of my aunt's, but they were well furnished by the lady of the house.

Mrs. Feingold, my foster mother, belonged to an organization called Pioneer Women. These ladies were supportive of Jewish causes and wanted to help those in other countries who had suffered persecution because of their faith. They were aware of the need to provide homes for the surviving children of the Holocaust. Many of the members of this idealistic group, with the agreement of their husbands, offered to share their homes with such children and provide them with all the necessities as if the children were their own, without expecting any compensation from the Jewish community. I had the good fortune to be the recipient of such generosity.

Mr. and Mrs. Feingold were a childless Jewish couple in their late fifties. They originally emigrated from Russia, and at home they conversed with each other in Yiddish, which originated as a form of German going back to the Middle Ages when German was the language of commerce in Europe. Once the Jewish population became dispersed, and often dispossessed, Jews in various countries continued speaking to each other in Yiddish, along with learning the language of the people among whom they now lived. They came to believe that Yiddish was the language of the Jews and Hebrew was too holy for everyday conversation.

My foster parents were unaware of my highly assimilated background and were surprised that I did not speak Yiddish, which in their eyes was a must for a Jewish girl. They immediately enrolled me in a Folks Shule, an elementary school with an after-school heritage program for Jewish children to learn Yiddish. I was surprised that I was to learn Yiddish, since I had presumed that in an English-speaking country, people would speak English. In addition, I felt quite insulted in the Folks Shule when they placed me in the beginner's class with six-year-olds. I soon decided that Yiddish was nothing more than a German dialect. I refused to go on the basis that I already knew German and that I was a grown person who shouldn't be in class with babies. My foster parents were upset that I said that their precious Yiddish was really German. However, they gave in when I started to talk to them in German, with a Yiddish accent, and they could understand me.

In some ways, both the Feingolds and I experienced culture shock, along with the many other problems of adjustment related to our differences in religious practices – or in my case the lack of them. For example, shortly after I moved in, it was the Jewish High Holy Days, one of which is Yom Kippur, a day when observant Jews fast and pray. I could not understand why these people would starve themselves when there was all that food in the house! The practice of keeping separate dishes for meat and dairy also made no sense to me. And I was not used to dressing and behaving like a lady, and preferred wearing slacks – a throwback to after the Soviets occupied Budapest, when it was safer for me to walk around looking like a boy than to be dressed as a girl.

I was also not much help in the kitchen, neither by training nor by inclination, as was expected of girls of my age. Even though Mrs. Feingold knew that I had not been brought up by my mother and had not been properly socialized in behaving like a lady, she was still critical of my independent behaviour and thought that I was uncouth. I, on the other hand, thought that dressing up in fancy clothes was a waste of time. But I kept my opinions to myself, partly because I did not have the language with which to express them, but mostly because I tried to please those nice people and not upset them again.

The Feingolds might not have had children of their own, but they treated their nieces and nephews as such, who lived in the second-floor suite of the little house the Feingolds lived in and in an identical house next door to them. In fact, Mrs. Feingold's eldest niece had just vacated the room I was in, because that year she got into nursing, which required that she live in residence next to the hospital. It was because her room became available that I was able to become part of the Feingold family at the very time I desperately needed a home.

Mr. Feingold was a sincerely good, deeply religious man. He worked very hard during the week – I think in the St. Lawrence fruit market. And although he was not a wealthy man, I found out after he died – from a black rabbi from New York who came to honour him at his funeral – that this good man had donated to the rabbi's Harlem synagogue a Torah that had been too expensive for their congregation to buy. There was never any mention of expenses when Mrs. Feingold went shopping with me to outfit me from head to toe in clothes similar to those the other young girls wore to school. When I asked for a bicycle for my sixteenth birthday – to their surprise, since to them it was a toy for children (though for me it was a way to right the wrong of that bicycle my cousin Rudi had stolen from me) – I got one without any questions asked! Mr. Feingold, whom I called "Daddy," gave me pocket money every week, and later, whenever my sister visited our home, he always slipped her some money, too. He and his wife, whom I called "Mommy," never had a cross word between them, although Mrs. Feingold had no trouble finding fault with most other people, including me.

Ilonka: Broken Promises

I was so glad to be on land and not feel seasick anymore. On the train, I sat by the window to see Canada. We passed lovely, picturesque sights. I saw acres of corn, lush green trees and fields of flowers painted in many colours. Nature is an artist! I could hardly wait to arrive in Toronto; I was so excited.

When Kati and I got to our destination, a trim social worker headed our way with a friendly smile on her face. She welcomed us pleasantly, shook our hands and spoke to us in English. One of the older kids translated for us because we couldn't understand a word she said. The lady told us that we were going to go shopping at Eaton's and be spruced up with new outfits. I guess we looked shabby, and we had to look attractive when we met the people who would be taking us in. The ladies who had reached out to the war orphans and were going to meet us belonged to a Jewish sisterhood. Their show of kindness and sympathy was reassuring, since I had just started to feel fearful and many questions had come to mind as I realized the problems I could have here, where nobody spoke Hungarian: How would I manage at school if I didn't understand English? How would I ask people on the street for directions if I got lost in a strange city?

Once we were in our temporary shelter in a former Jewish library, ladies from the sisterhood arrived to choose one of us to take home. I hated being scrutinized, but the ladies all smiled and we all smiled back. Nobody wanted to take two sisters, but I was chosen alone right away and went to the home of a Polish family with two sons. One of the boys was two years older than me and the other two years younger. Mr. and Mrs. Goldberg spoke Yiddish to each other and English to the boys and to me, except that I did not understand what they said. Without communication, being there was awkward, especially when I called the lady "Mama" and the man "Papa" and I did not even know them. Soon I relaxed, because even without being able to communicate, everyone kept smiling and seemed very nice. I got a room of my own, which used to belong to the younger boy. This reassured me that I would have a place in this nice family, and I felt pleased, because never before had I had a room to myself. I thought that the promise made to Aunt Margaret about Kati and me moving to Canada would really come true.

Mama Goldberg signed me up for Grade 7, since that was the right grade for my age. When I was introduced, all the kids looked at me as a curiosity because I could not speak English. I felt they were thinking that I was stupid. I sat for hours day after day in the class without learning anything, since everything that was taught, except for gym and music, in which I could participate easily, was in English, and I didn't understand anything the teacher said. In my boredom, I started to draw cartoons, sometimes of naked women. A boy behind me grabbed my drawing from my desk and passed it around. From that day on the kids in my class showed lots of interest in me. They befriended me, wanted to teach me English and walked home with me. During recess, I taught them acrobatics: handstands, the splits and the bridge. I even showed them dance steps: hop, shuffle, hop shuffle and tap. The kids were impressed and we bonded as we taught each other what we knew best. I was invited to birthday parties, and as I gained acceptance by my new friends at school, I started to feel happy.

But at home, I sensed that something was wrong by the way the family behaved toward me without even saying anything. I felt sad and unloved, resented by the boys and ignored by Papa Goldberg. I cried when I was alone in my room, because I missed being with my sister, I missed my old friends, I missed my aunt Margaret's love and my uncle Vili's chicken paprikash. The Goldbergs were fine, and polite, but not truly loving like my aunt or my mother had been.

One day the Goldbergs told the social worker that they had to have my room for a relative who needed a helping hand, and she should find me another home. They did not seem to care what would happen to me. I thought I was being sent away because I cried a lot and they did not want a sad child. My sister told me that it was not my fault, that the boys must have been jealous of the attention their mother gave me and that Mr. Goldberg probably resented the inconvenience and extra expense of a growing girl. All I knew was that Mr. and Mrs. Goldberg were not a real mama and papa, just pretend, and I learned what it was to be disillusioned and not to trust.

My social worker next found a home for me with a young, immigrant Polish couple who spoke Yiddish – I guess because my social worker assumed, incorrectly, that I would be able to communicate in Yiddish with them. Unlike the Goldbergs, who were not paid to keep me and who were to treat me as their own child, this family saw me as a tenant and received money for room and board each month for my keep. I no longer had a room of my own but slept in the same room as their four-year-old girl. She was sent to bed earlier than me, but when I was to go to bed, I was not allowed to turn on the light even to get undressed or set my hair in bobby pins, for fear I might wake their child. Food, which was so important to me even when I was not hungry, was carefully measured, and a generous amount was first served to the little girl before I got any. When I told Kati this, she got very angry.

Weekdays I went to a new school, continuing the second term of Grade 7, but on the weekends I was supposed to stay in the apartment to babysit so the young couple could have some free time to enjoy each other's company. I didn't get much chance to see my sister, or even some of the Hungarian-speaking kids with whom I had formed friendships during our long trip from Budapest. I felt lonely, and being in a new school again, with new classmates in a new neighbourhood, I felt like a fish out of water. I was unhappier than I had been with Mama and Papa Goldberg, because I lost even the hope that I could become accepted as part of a real family, so far away from my own. I knew that I had no choice if I was not to be sent away for complaining, and I tried to fit in among these strangers by smiling a lot, while my heart was aching.

I didn't know that my sister, who by this time could speak English fairly well, had gone to Miss Spivak and told on the young couple. I am not sure what was discussed, but at the end of the school year I was sent to a B'nai Brith overnight summer camp, and after camp I was placed in a third foster home. The arrangements were similar to those with the young couple, but the house was only a ten-minute walk from Kati, who by this time had had her name anglicized and was called Kitty. This family also lived in a small two-bedroom apartment, just like the young couple before. I had to share a room with their active three-year-old boy, and even though the Jewish Child and Family Service paid for my keep, once again I was expected to babysit.

The lady of the house was warm and at times seemed caring, but her husband was cold and rude. He was a Holocaust survivor; his native language was German, and I heard rumours from my Hungarian-speaking friends that he had been a kapo in a concentration camp, which meant that even though he was Jewish, he was in charge of controlling the other inmates in exchange for privileges from the Nazi guards. There was never any proof of this, but from the cold and at times insulting way that he behaved toward me, I had no difficulty believing it. Eventually, I no longer complained even to my sister about his rude way of talking to me, or about my lack of privacy, at the age of almost fourteen, sleeping in the same room as a little boy. I was glad I could see Kitty often after school, and I could see my friends on the weekends too, so I did not want to move.

In my third foster home, I was never really comfortable or considered part of the family. Still, at least living near my sister's home was a great comfort to me because I knew that she was one person who for sure loved me for myself just like our mother had. As I started to speak and understand more English, that also helped. I began to feel more comfortable with the kids at school in Grade 8, where I again was appreciated for the funny caricatures I drew of naked ladies. I liked being at the B'nai Brith summer camp because it was a lot of fun, like the camp I went to from the Miha. During the school year I saw some of the same kids I met at camp, because in this third foster home, I was also allowed to go to a B'nai Brith youth group during the weekends and holidays. There I became friends with a few girls my age, although some of the girls in the group looked down on me and treated me as an oddity because of my funny accent. They may also have felt that way because the boys in the group thought I was pretty and glamorously different from these girls because of my accent, and they liked to dance with me better because I could dance very well. I decided that even though I did not care for being in the same room with the noisy little boy or listening to the rude talk of his father, if I could ignore those two, living in Canada was not going to be so terrible, and I would be okay.

~

REFUGEE CHILD

Walking on a tightrope without a net,
If I make a sudden move, could fall and break my neck.
Coming across the ocean with a group of orphan kids,
I hoped to find a loving family and a safe place to live.
Canada was a strange place, I tried to adopt their ways.
People were suspicious 'cause where we came from was different
      than theirs.
Couldn't speak English, that was a big drawback.

Couldn't communicate, which left me frustrated, mad.
I arrived in Canada at the age of thirteen, orphaned at the age of nine.
I was dependent on others for survival, felt humiliated and cried.
When I was placed in my first foster home, I was excited to find a
permanent place.
But I became disillusioned, was sent away with shame on my face.
In the second foster place Yiddish and Polish were spoken.
There was no pretense of care for me, or show of love, for which I
was hoping.
I did not belong there and I sensed that much,
I was an intruder in their family's life.
In the third place they needed a built-in sitter so they could go more
often out of town.
I had stopped trusting people's motives by then, and become sad and
withdrawn.
I walked on tiptoe day in and day out, trying not to offend or step
on any toes
Hoping that by my best behaviour they wouldn't show me to the
door.
I shed bitter tears in the silence of the night
When no one could see the pain in my heart.
Without those who loved me I felt all alone, and came to realize
That while I still had dreams for the future like any other child,
Without parental love and backing, they would not materialize.

~

I think that the social worker who placed me in three such insensitive environments must have thought of me not as a young girl in need of care, love and guidance, but as just one of the cases in her portfolio. I am sure that if she had thought of me as her own little sister who was only thirteen years old and separated from her family and home, she would have taken more care in finding out how I was coping and how

I could get more support both academically and emotionally.

I now realize that some of my misery was caused not just by the social worker's lack of awareness or by the indifference of the families with whom I was placed. With my predisposition to be timid and my painful concern for the opinion of others, I too contributed to my difficulties in adapting to the constant moves I had to cope with. I was even afraid to help myself to food from the refrigerator, no matter how hungry I felt, and I wouldn't complain about a nail in my shoe that constantly cut into my flesh, for fear that I would be sent away again for costing the family too much money if they had to give me more food or get me another pair of shoes. I was also still suffering from shock at the unexpected forced separation from my sister, for whose sake I had left my home at Aunt Margaret's in the first place. In addition, every move the first year of my life in Canada caused me more and more stress because it involved not only a change in language but also the need to adapt to the ways of the variety of people I was introduced to, both in the foster homes and in the new schools I was sent to. Unfortunately, as much as I wanted to be loved and accepted, I never bonded with any member of my foster families. Whenever I was introduced as Ellen, the refugee child, I cringed. It made me feel like a charity case. I thought my foster parents said this to show people how charitable they were for taking me into their home, when I knew that they would not have kept me if the agency had not paid them. After my heart was broken by the Goldberg family, I never trusted another family again and always felt like a person who is outside the house, not able to enter and just looking in.

During my four years as a foster child, I developed some methods and philosophies that helped me cope. I learned to keep my mouth shut and not express my opinions so as not to make waves. I learned that if there was an argument in the family between the mother and the father, I should always stay neutral and never side with either because if I did, the other would resent it and get mad at me. I learned to mind my own business and not expect any love from them.

I developed a guide that I called my "inner compass." I compared myself to the ship at sea on which I had travelled to this new world. Just as a ship sailing through the calm and at times turbulent waters of the ocean without a compass can be guided by the stars instead, I learned to direct myself without the guidance of parental counsel, or love and care. I took direction from my sister, as well as from my peers and teachers at school, and kept on learning and propelling myself through each day as I progressed through life. Reflecting on their teaching and examples, I created my own compass to navigate the currents and storms of my life, trying to use good judgment to make decisions on my own and arrive with self-respect at the port of maturity.

Kitty: Lucky Accident

I did not mind calling the Feingolds "Mom" and "Dad" and did not think I was dishonouring my parents or forgetting them, since they would remain in my heart forever. I thought that through being with this family, my parents were somehow protecting me. Had I remained in Hungary, as wonderful as my aunt Margaret was, I would have been elbow deep in grease and dead chickens, selling poultry at the open market in all kinds of weather. Instead, here in Canada I was sent to school, my most favourite place in the world.

Bloor Collegiate was located near our house. I was first taken there by my foster mother, and was interviewed by the principal himself, Mr. Noble. I understood when he asked me my name and how old I was. I answered carefully, supplying the version of my name that had been newly given to me by the immigration authorities: "My name is Catherine Mozes-Nagy and I am fifteen years old." He responded, "You are?" And I answered, "I are."

I was placed in the lowest grade in the school: Grade 9. Just to make sure I would not get lost on the way to school, Mrs. Feingold arranged with a neighbour to have her daughter, Marjorie, who was in my class, walk with me every day. This sturdy girl came for me every morning and conscientiously accompanied me – in silence – probably forgoing walking with her friends. I hated silence, and after a while, once my vocabulary increased, we started to talk.

Going to high school was an interesting experience. First of all, there were boys *and* girls in the school – and in the same classroom! What made me feel even more aware that this was a very different kind of school from the one I was used to was that the teachers called us by our first names. I was to be called Catherine – I could hardly spell it, let alone pronounce it – but I immediately corrected anyone who called me that and said, "My name is Kati." People smiled and called me Kitty. I did not realize that this was what people here called baby cats. I didn't mind – I was happy that I was no longer addressed as Mozes. Being called by my first name also signified to me that the teachers were my friends. As I later found out, the staff at this school felt sympathetic toward the young people who had arrived from Europe and tried their best to help them through the initial adjustment.

Nevertheless, as much as I was glad to be at school, I found plenty of difficulties. I managed to get by in mathematics and French, but the other classes made me feel tired because I truly strained to understand what was being taught. For me, who was used to knowing the answers to the questions, always being quiet because I didn't was an added strain. When I got home, my foster mother, not understanding the stress I was experiencing, would complain that a girl my age should not always feel so tired.

November 14, 1948, was my sixteenth birthday, and I felt fortunate. Although, for obvious reasons, none of the kids at school except Marjorie bothered to talk to me, at the Feingolds' the phone always kept ringing with callers asking for me. The other young Hungarians who had come to Canada with me had adjustment problems as well, and to find support, we turned to each other for friendship. So for the first time in my life, I experienced popularity by default. Mr. and Mrs. Feingold, besides giving me a bicycle as a birthday present, said that I could have a birthday party and invite anybody I wished. This birthday party, too, was a first in my life.

The best present I got from one of the boys was a slightly used book entitled *Forever Amber*. I am sure my ship brother had no idea what kind of story this book told, or that because of its risqué content it had been banned in fourteen states and warned against from many pulpits as an instrument of the devil. As far as I was concerned, it was God-sent. By this time, I had acquired a reasonable amount of English to use in everyday conversations in a broken way. Starved for books, I used my English-Hungarian dictionary and started to read this story about a beautiful girl who was abandoned and penniless, far away from her home, but who managed to survive and be successful, even during terrible times such as the Great Plague and the Great Fire of London. I could understand her feelings of abandonment and distress, and although I did not identify with her sexual exploits, which helped her become the most powerful woman of her time in England, I was interested in these exploits, which I considered most instructive.

With the exception of being concerned about my sister, who was treated as a charity case by the people who housed her as well as by her social worker, whom I continued to call and complain to, I didn't do much but read. My sister was a far sweeter, more accommodating child than I was, but she had difficulty in her foster homes. I think, in the first home, the problem might not have been Ilonka – now Ellen – but the sons, who may have been jealous and didn't want to share their parents' attention with this intruder, and possibly their father, who did not necessarily want the extra expense of supporting a growing young girl. Nobody ever said this, but after my sister started to form bonds with her foster mother and some of her new classmates, she was informed that by December she would have to go to another foster home because the family needed her room for some cousins newly arriving from Europe. Ellen was heartbroken and kept telling me that she had not done anything wrong, and she didn't know why they were sending her away.

Taking time only for eating, sleeping and an occasional attempt at homework, I spent every waking moment avidly reading *Forever Amber*. Without being aware of it, my vocabulary, comprehension and ability to express myself in complex literary ways grew tremendously. My foster parents were impressed that even during the Christmas holidays I would spend hours in my room, just "studying." When I returned to school in January, my teachers noticed the great improvement, which showed in my class participation and my written answers. They thought I was very smart, and I thought so, too.

During my walks to school with Marjorie, now that we talked I found out that she was turning thirteen. I knew that to be in Grade 9 you had to be at least fourteen, so I asked her how it was possible for her to be in this class when she was so young. She told me that she had been an excellent student in elementary school and she was allowed to skip a grade. This seemed like a great idea for me as well. I went to the principal's office and asked to talk to Mr. Noble. This kind gentleman, who had seen me in September for admission, took time to speak with me in his office. With my newly acquired vocabulary, I told him, "I don't want to be in Grade 9 any longer. I want to skip." When he asked for my reason, I told him that I was older than the rest of the students in my grade, and I had a great deal of knowledge that they did not have. Mr. Noble smiled patiently and said that he would certainly consider my proposal if, during the rest of the year, I could prove to him what I said by getting very good grades. His encouragement motivated me to do my best – not to show up my fellow students, as I had done in Hungary, but to give myself a chance to make up for the years I was held back in school there.

I am not sure if, at the end of the school year, I really would have been allowed to skip a whole grade of high school, not only because my marks by the end of the year were not exceptional, but also because this practice was only allowed then in the elementary program. It took another accident of fate to come to my help.

⁓

By June 1949, a lot had happened in the ten months since our arrival in Canada. After I complained to the Jewish Family and Child Service about breaking their promise to make sure that my younger sister was properly cared for in Canada, the social worker compromised by finding Ellen a place that at least was close to where I lived. Since sending her back to Hungary was not a good option, and no loving family was eager to adopt a fourteen-year-old, the new place seemed like the best solution.

My Grade 9 final exams were in June. I had to write all the exams because the papers I had written in December when I could not yet speak English had pulled down my average. I studied ferociously, hoping to prove to Mr. Noble that I deserved to skip a grade. By the time the English exam came, I was relieved that it was scheduled for the afternoon; I would be able to sleep in, since I had studied late at night. I was wrong. At eight thirty that morning, the telephone rang. My foster mother woke me up and told me that I needed to be in class because the English exam was starting and all the students were seated. I jumped on my bike, and as I pedalled at great speed, rushing to the school, I remember pulling out the curlers from my hair and throwing them away. I have no idea what I did with the bicycle, but I got into the classroom just as the students were starting to write, and was handed an exam paper. Without wasting another second, I began to answer the questions.

The first part of the exam asked us to interpret a poem, and the poet's feelings and meaning. I liked the questions and had little difficulty answering them. The second part was not that hard either. We were to read a short story and write a summary, or précis. After that we had to fix some sentences with incorrect grammar. By this time, I had read *Forever Amber* at least twice, so I was quite familiar with proper grammatical forms in English and I did not worry about my answers. It was the next part of the exam that gave me trouble. We were asked to comment on a play by Shakespeare we never even studied in class. I put up my hand and told the supervising teacher that this was not a fair question because we had never learned about this play. She asked me what grade I was in. I told her I was a Grade 9 student. She then said that I had been given a Grade 11 paper by mistake when I entered the room late. She took my half-finished exam paper and told me to wait in the office. The secretary called my foster family and explained the mistake, and said that I would be given lunch at school and allowed to write my proper exam under supervision in the afternoon. In the meantime, Mrs. Brooks, the Grade 11 English teacher, took the time to mark my Grade 11 exam. Apparently, I passed all the parts that I answered. The following day, Mr. Noble called my foster parents and told them I would be placed in Grade 11 come September.

~

That summer, I discovered how Canadians live during the summer. They go to cottages by the lake in extended family groups, cook a lot of food, get wet in the cold lake and then sit in the sun to dry. Life by the lake in a small summer cottage was dull for me, even though there were a few young people close to my age and next to our cottage was a small summer family resort called The Tides Hotel, which seemed to have lots of people coming and going. I have never been a very social person, and I did not form friendships with those youngsters. The closest I got to conversation was with one of the boys whom I asked for help catching up with mathematics and German. I was sure to be behind in those subjects since I was skipping Grade 10. The group's social activities were beyond my appreciation, and I found nothing in common with anyone in the group to talk about.

On top of this boredom, Mr. Feingold, a well-intentioned romantic, kept showing up with various Hungarian-speaking ship brothers of mine in tow whenever he joined the family for the weekend, and I was stuck with some of these guys, whom I hadn't trusted in the first place. One might have thought that, given our common background and history, we would at least have talked about that. I recall reading André Stein's book *Broken Silence*, which explained why we didn't discuss what had happened to us and to the members of our families, even among ourselves. I now understand that we all tried to block out those experiences and memories, and only many decades later do some victims find the ability and courage to speak about their most painful past experiences.

~

While Ellen and I finally started to adjust to the ways of our new world, life in Hungary under the communist regime grew worse for many people, including our family. My cousin Rudi, now married and with a small child, decided that he would much rather be elsewhere and left his wife and child illegally to come to the land of gold, Canada. It was the practice of the communist government that if it could not punish the culprit who defected, it would punish an innocent member of his family. My poor elderly uncle Vili, who still suffered from pain in his legs, was thrown into jail for having a "bad" son. Uncle Latzi, whose marriage had broken up from the stress of losing baby Gyurika, also joined the many who wanted to immigrate to Canada. It seemed that Ellen and I had written enough positive things about this new world, and we became the pioneers of our family. Both cousin Rudi and Uncle Latzi, with his new wife, eventually ended up settling in Toronto because Ellen and I were already here.

Ellen: Out in the World

I no sooner got used to Grade 8 in my new school and formed friendships with a few of my classmates than the school year ended and it was time for us to part. Most of the students in my class were going on to Grade 9 in high school. Unlike Kati, I was not allowed to because I had to be prepared for earning a living by the time I was sixteen years old. The summer at B'nai Brith camp that year was great fun, since this time I knew many of the kids there from the year before, and by now I could speak English quite easily.

Once summer was over, Miss Spivak enrolled me in Givins Commercial School. Thrust unprepared into another new environment, I had to rely on my inner compass, which guided me, to protect myself and others who were as vulnerable as me. Most of the girls at school were kind, but there were also those who were quite mean and ganged up on some of the more defenceless kids. I recall two girls in particular who were harassing a young girl much smaller than they were. I witnessed them tormenting her. In the presence of some bigger boys in the schoolyard, these girls held down the smaller girl, pulled her skirt up to her head and exposed her body for the guys to see. Ordinarily, I was quite timid and minded my own business, but I remembered how I felt when I was bullied as a little girl in Hungary, and I thought that this was wrong. I didn't care if the bullying girls would go after me as well; I just went to the office and reported to the principal what the girls were doing. They stopped bothering the small girl, and even though they kept giving me dirty looks all through that year, they never did anything to me to get revenge – probably because they knew that I would tell on them again.

It made no sense for an immigrant child with only two years in the country to be placed in this school. Nobody who made this choice of study for me had considered that although I may have learned to read, I had not yet had enough time to learn how to spell properly. I was being trained to be a secretary and our subjects included penmanship, shorthand and typing. I had had two years of absolutely useless education that had prepared me for nothing before I was told that now I was old enough to start earning my keep by getting a job.

The only bright spot in my life then was the B'nai Brith youth group. We had no homework at the commercial school, so every weekend I could attend activities and parties with other young people in the group. I loved going, and became friends with some of the girls who had interests like mine in show business and dancing. In a kind of community centre, we played records, danced and put on talent shows. I was actively involved in a Ping-Pong tournament, which I won, and I became the star of a Valentine dance contest where my partner lifted me up high while I did a back bend as we danced. Some of the girls who had tried to get the attention of David, most popular boy in the group, were not too appreciative that he, the president of our club, asked *me* to be his date for the most special dance of the year because he was impressed by my dancing.

During the week, I was forced to face reality. Looking in the want ads of the newspaper, I found a job as a waitress in a Hungarian restaurant. I thought that because I could speak both English and Hungarian and I loved cooking and food, this was an ideal place for me to work. Perhaps it would have been, considering my less-than-superior secretarial skills, except that once when I was alone in the kitchen with the cook, who was the owner of the establishment, he asked me with a big grin on his face, "Are you still a virgin?" I was quite upset and insulted because I knew his question was rude and disrespectful. I went to complain to the cashier, who was his wife. She did not sympathize but glared at me and asked, "Well, are you?" I am still proud of my decision to quit that job, even though I was not sure I would be able to get another before the rent for my room was due.

The want ads came to my rescue with a job in a factory. Lots of young girls worked there in an unventilated room, gluing the lining into purses, then sewing it in as well. No one was rude to me, but the place was bad for the health of the workers. The threads we used for sewing kept cutting my fingers, and the fumes from the glue made me dizzy and nauseous. I don't think I lasted longer than a week.

I was concerned about finding a job that I would be able to keep, but I did not give up. I quite quickly got a job selling Israel Bonds. I was to go door to door with a list of names of Jewish people who might be interested in supporting the young State of Israel. Many doors were closed abruptly in my face. At one place a lady thought that perhaps I was a beggar. She felt sorry for me and handed me two hard-boiled eggs in case I was hungry. My sense of self-respect did not allow me to stay at a job in which every time I knocked on a door I could meet with annoyance, distrust or pity. My inner compass told me not to give up and to keep looking.

As it turned out, Kitty's friend Lillian found herself a summer job in a resort called Taub's that needed not one but three young girls. Lillian became the counsellor for the guests' children, Kitty worked as the nanny for the owners' children and I sat at the front desk as the hotel receptionist and secretary. My foster parents advised me not to take this job because it was just for the summer, but Kitty said that my foster parents didn't care that I had an opportunity to be in a nice place with my sister; they just wanted to keep getting rent without interruption and didn't want to lose their live-in babysitter. I decided to go to the resort because of the chance to be with my sister again, and I did not mind if I had to go searching for another job when summer was over. All three of us were happy that summer; we had a wonderful time and even got paid at the end of the season. The only thing I missed from the city was the company of David, who by now considered us going steady.

Once summer was over, I went back to my foster home, but I did not live there for much longer. My uncle Latzi, who had recently come to Canada, rented a house with his second wife and their baby. They were renting out rooms to help them manage, and they preferred to have me in their home instead of someone else. I still needed to find a job right away because I had to pay rent there as well, since they needed the income, but I would be with part of my family. It was also great to live there because I had my own room at last. In addition, I liked playing with my new little cousin, and my new auntie cooked delicious Hungarian food. To add to my happiness, I finally got lucky with a job as a receptionist in the office of an optometrist. He appreciated that I had had previous experience at the summer resort as a receptionist, but unfortunately, my wages for this job, as with the others before, were very low. I barely managed to pay for my keep at my uncle's home, and I had hardly any money left for anything else. Still, the job was easy, my boss was pleasant and I liked dealing with the people who came to him for eyeglasses.

In order to have extra money for such luxuries as streetcar fare or clothes and movies, I had to find an additional part-time job. I went back to the want ads in the newspapers and I had good luck again. A new dance studio was opening up and auditioning talented people to train as dance instructors evenings and weekends. Of the twenty people who auditioned for the job, I was one of the five chosen. Not only did the people who hired me like the way I danced and looked, they liked my accent, which was an added advantage because it seemed glamorous in that environment.

I loved this job! I could dance every evening and get paid for doing what I liked best. Our trainers taught us many variations of the different kinds of ballroom dancing. I was successful and a lot of people requested me as their instructor, because besides being quite an expert at dancing, I was patient with the students who were not as well coordinated. Unfortunately, as time went on, our supervisors pressured us to flatter the students and, no matter how poorly they danced, to tell them that if they signed up for more classes, they could become exceptional dancers. We were supposed to talk them into more and more lessons by what I considered trickery.

Just like my sister while at the Miha, I too could not pretend and say what I knew was not true, and just like her, I too left a place I liked very much. But I felt better, because I had held on to my convictions and self-respect.

Kitty: Most Favourite Place

While Ellen did her best in her new world, I did my best in mine. Grade 11 was not easy, though I had not expected it to be. The class I was placed in was for advanced students who eventually would go to university. Besides science and mathematics, we were to study German, French and Latin in addition to English. I thought four languages were a bit too much for me, so I asked if I could drop Latin. The guidance counsellor said that would be allowed. In place of Latin I could have a spare, or I could take a typing class in the adjoining commercial school. Happily, I chose typing, and the skill has proven useful and practical – especially when I began writing my memoirs.

I thought all my teachers were excellent. On the many occasions when I had trouble understanding what they said, they were kind enough to take the time to explain some concept that I might have missed by skipping Grade 10. By the time I got home from a full day of intense concentration, all I wanted to do was have a nap before dinner. Mommy Feingold was quite annoyed at this show of "laziness." Because she had not had any formal education – I suspected that she could not read or write, through no fault of her own – she had no sympathy for, and little understanding of, the stress I subjected myself to by taking those new languages all at once; not to mention that at home I continued to irritate her by speaking German instead of Yiddish.

I no longer had Marjorie as my walking companion. Her family had moved to the northern part of Toronto, and she now went to a high school in that area. To escape Mommy's caustic criticisms, I did not go home directly after school but to the home of Lillian, a new friend of mine. Lillian's family owned a corner grocery store, and they lived above it. Lillian was a bit of a rebel herself, and so she had been kindly escorted out of Harbord Collegiate, the school of her choice, to attend the school assigned to students who lived in my area. Lillian was actually a year ahead of me, but she had missed a couple of required subjects at her former school and had to complete them at the Grade 11 level. Perhaps because Lillian was somewhat untraditional, she befriended this strong-accented foreign student: me. She and I often ate lunch together, and when we had a bit of money, we would go to the nearby café and order one piece of lemon meringue pie to share, since we could not afford two. When I told Lillian that I desperately needed to sleep or rest after school but this was totally unacceptable at my home, Lil suggested that I crash at her place. For months, until I got acclimatized to Grade 11 and caught up to the other students' level, I would go to sleep at Lillian's apartment for an hour or so, then go home to have supper. By January of that year I was much more relaxed and no longer needed the extra rest, but I remained forever grateful to Lillian and her kind parents for tolerating this intrusion into their home by a strange friend of their daughter's.

I passed Grade 11 with fairly good marks, and with summer now here, the Feingold family, along with all the aunts and their children, would be going back to the cottage, with its less-than-exciting activities. I had a great idea of how to escape both the teenage social life and the ship brothers that Daddy Feingold planned to import again as visitors for me. I thought that perhaps I could get a job next door to the cottage at The Tides Hotel.

Mr. Tom Brown must have had a sense of humour. He hired me, a girl with a strong Hungarian accent, to answer the telephone, make announcements on the loudspeaker and be the general secretary for his office at his resort. Since so recently after the war there were not yet many immigrants in the country, and since those who were here generally did not use loudspeakers, I think I was a bit of a novelty. Every time I announced something or an upcoming event, several people came running to the office to find out what I had just said!

There was not much secretarial work to do. The staff was actually part of the entertainment for the guests, who were mostly couples and their children. The resort was located on Lake Simcoe, and it offered an opportunity for families to just enjoy the summer without cooking or cleaning. I had a great time interacting with both the guests and the staff, mostly young men who worked as waiters and were putting themselves through college by getting tips. The hotel also had a young master of ceremonies who made sure nobody got bored, even on rainy days. I recall that one evening the staff, including me, had to put on a talent show. I had no trouble singing and dancing in front of an audience, what with the training my father had given me singing on the tabletops of cafés when I was a young child. I surprised everybody with my comic performance and stole the show. That summer experience helped me develop more things in common with young Canadians my age and become more comfortable with them. With Lillian's encouragement, I finally began to see members of the opposite sex not just as potential threats, but also as people who might be fun to be with and maybe really like.

⁓

That year, 1950, was not an easy one for Mr. and Mrs. Feingold. Daddy had a heart attack and we all had to face how fragile life can be. He quit smoking on the spot and stopped working, which probably was not an easy adjustment for a hard-working man. Mommy Feingold was scared and so was I, because I had learned to love this gentle, kind man, who, even though he was not my real father, behaved as if he was. Soon we could relax, because he got better. Life went back to normal, and I did my best to please my foster parents by trying my hardest at school and attempting to help Mommy in the kitchen whenever she allowed me near her kosher dishes. My ignorance of *kashrut* was an issue for my foster mother – she worried that I could possibly make her dishes *treif*, unclean.

Unlike my sister, I had little time or interest in dating or romance, nor did I care that I was not included in the social activities of my peers. This changed suddenly that spring. During my routine checkup at the dentist's office, there was a young man, a patient, sitting in the dentist's chair. Once the dentist finished looking after him, I had my turn. When my checkup was over, the young man was still in the waiting room – waiting for me. He walked me home and on the way we talked. Harvey was eighteen years old, like me, and the year before he had been out of school because his father had died and his mother and two younger brothers needed Harvey's paycheque to support them. Even after missing a year of school, he was still a year ahead of me, and was serious about doing his best in Grade 13. In spite of a heavy course load, he also worked on the weekends in a fast-food restaurant as a cook, and gave all the money he made to his mother. I was impressed by his unselfish actions to help his family and the gentle way that he talked. When he asked me on a date, I was happy to go, and very soon we decided that we were in love and would be going steady.

That summer, Harvey already had a job lined up for him as an encyclopedia salesman, and I had committed myself to a job in another summer resort. I would very much have liked to stay in Toronto to be near my boyfriend, but I also looked forward to spending the summer with my sister, Ellen, and my friend Lillian at Taub's Lodge. As it turned out, this separation was a good idea, because Harvey's mother was unhappy that her son was no longer totally devoted to providing for her family's needs.

At Taub's my sister was the secretary and I was to look after Mrs. Taub's three children. Mr. Taub had died unexpectedly that winter, and his poor wife was left with the responsibility of running the lodge or losing everything. Her three girls were seven-year-old Chayethel, five-year-old Meirah and eighteen-month-old Neshama. These children were traumatized by the loss of their dad and the consequent separation from their mother, who was now busy making sure that she would not lose the resort because of poor management.

As a nanny for the three little girls, I was expected to act like a substitute parent. I did not need to cook the meals, but I ate with the children and I had to do everything else a mother must do, including changing diapers and washing them out by hand, because that many years ago disposable diapers had only just been invented and were not yet common.

During the day Chayethel was in the program run by Lillian for the guests' children, but Neshama often cried because she wanted her mommy, and Meirah was at times easily frustrated, had tantrums and often tried to do the opposite of what was asked of her. Having longed for my own mother, I was sympathetic, and that helped in eventually getting the little ones to feel more comfortable with me. But I missed Harvey and I did not have fun being a nanny. I was really not mature enough to appreciate the importance of my role as a nanny to three children who until then were used to having their mother look after them. The job was completely outside any of my experiences, with the exception of looking after my sister when I too was a child. It was also quite different from the work I had done the previous summer as a secretary-receptionist at The Tides resort. Nevertheless, the experience was great preparation for becoming a teacher and, later, a parent.

Then once again the summer was over. Mr. and Mrs. Feingold were glad to have me back home and they were proud of me going into Grade 13. Students had to get nine credits to complete that grade, and Harvey was a great help in teaching me how to study most efficiently for exams. He could have gone to any university of his choice, but because of his family's financial needs, he chose to become a chartered accountant. I do not think that the program still exists, but at the time people could obtain their certification by working in the office of a chartered accountant. His salaried job was considered part of the course, which he was to study on his own time and then write exams for to prove his knowledge. That way Harvey could support his family and acquire a profession at the same time. Just as he had been an excellent student in high school, Harvey was an outstanding student here, and he received the gold medal twice in accounting for having the highest standing in the program.

I had an inkling that Harvey was not as seriously committed to me as I was to him. Having completed Grade 13, I was again looking for a summer job, especially because I did not want to take any more allowance from Daddy, who was not working. With the help of my experience as a nanny, I found a well-paying job as a counsellor in a day camp in the city. Harvey was against me staying in the city for the summer. He thought I should be away at the lodge again. When I asked him why he would prefer me not to work in Toronto when he himself would be staying in the city, he finally confessed that he did not wish to go steady anymore. He cried as he professed that he loved me, but he said he could not be committed to me because his mother did not think it was a good idea.

I was both hurt and furious. I thought that his mother was terribly unfair and Harvey should not be such a wimp but act like a man and stand by me if he really cared. I now understand that her opposing a lifetime commitment between two nineteen-year-olds, no matter how responsible they are, was not totally based on self-interest, as I had then thought. As an adult I can see that such a commitment can lead to problems for a young couple when neither of them has a penny, or any training for earning a living. I magnanimously decided that I would give Harvey a chance to change his mind, but only until September, after which time if he did not call, I would show him and go out with other boys.

Actually, Harvey did me a favour by breaking up, because until then I was not spending as much time on my studies as I should have been. Now, with no other distraction, I finally started to concentrate in earnest on preparing for the final Grade 13 exams, and applied through my guidance counsellor to go to school to be trained as an elementary school teacher. At the end of that school year, although only nine exams were required to complete Grade 13, I was to write eleven including three languages, chemistry and three areas of mathematics. Using the method Harvey had taught me for preparing for exams, I passed all of them. I was accepted into teaching school, provided my personal interview was satisfactory.

In 1952, all at once, the many children born in Canada after World War II became old enough to start going to school. This was the baby boom generation. The Ontario Ministry of Education was caught in the dilemma of finding enough classrooms and teachers to provide education for this large number of children as quickly as possible. That year, to become an elementary school teacher, a person did not need to pay tuition for the classes nor have a university education; one was accepted for a one-year training program right from Grade 12. With just one year of preparation, a seventeen- or eighteen-year-old was then allowed to teach in an elementary school classroom. At nineteen, I was at least a year older than most of the other applicants and, with my Grade 13 completed, better qualified than most of them. I had no doubt that I would be accepted.

But the personal interview did not go well. As soon as I started to speak, it was obvious that the interviewers were not prepared for the heavy Hungarian accent that I myself could not hear. Given that I was more qualified than many of the students, and not wanting to appear prejudiced, I suppose, they accepted me, with the proviso that by December I drastically modify my accent; if it was not to their satisfaction at that time, they would have a right to ask me to leave the program. To me this seemed a set-up for failure, since I could not imagine how I could possibly change my way of speaking in three and a half months.

I thought it was unfair of them to lead me on about accepting me, then make me leave in the middle of the year with nowhere to go. I went to Miss Frazer, my guidance counsellor at Bloor Collegiate, and told her what had happened. She agreed with me and said that she would help me apply for a bursary to the University of Toronto. A year there would give me even better qualifications and additional time to modify my accent. I called the teaching school and told them I planned to act on their advice; I would work on my accent and would be taking an additional year to do it, and I asked them to please hold my application for the year, after which I would like to try my interview again. The board agreed and told me to set up another interview in the spring of the following year.

In defiance of Harvey's advice to go back to the out-of-town summer resort, I became a counsellor at Camp Robin Hood, in Toronto's Sherwood Park. For good measure, I also got two jobs at the Canadian National Exhibition for the last ten days of the summer. I liked my job at the day camp, but my greatest time was working at the CNE. During the day I served hamburgers and deli sandwiches at Dinty Moore's – eating them too, of course – and after five o'clock I drew portraits of the public for an established artist, who provided the space and equipment for a group of us in one of the main buildings of the CNE, for a share of our earnings. I was so busy I hardly had any time or energy to think of Harvey, although I still hoped to hear from him before September.

He did not call, but Miss Frazer did, with the good news that I had received a substantial bursary to attend University College at the University of Toronto full-time. To my dismay, Mom and Dad Feingold did not want me to go any further in higher education. They said that they were worried I would become so smart no one would want to marry me and that if I went against their wishes, I would not be able to stay with them any more. I think I cried and asked them, "Do you really want me to give back all this money?" Looking at it from that point of view, they relented and said it would be all right for me to go to university at least for that year.

During the previous four years, while I had been attending high school, many of the young people I had come with to Canada had different experiences and expectations from mine. When we landed in Halifax, most of them were at least seventeen years old; some were even a few years older but pretended to be seventeen to get a chance at a new life away from the horrors of the past. Unlike me, they lived in rented rooms, were not too involved with their hosts as part of a family and found comfort in each other's company. As soon as most of my ship brothers learned English, they found a job, became capable of supporting themselves and got married to other young Holocaust survivors or to young Canadian women. Compared with them and with the girls in the group, who saw happiness as being married and creating a home of their own, I was a late bloomer. Until I met Harvey, I had never even thought of being in love, and even when I thought I was, I could not imagine myself as a housewife. My interests were school and becoming an artist. Getting a chance to continue my studies was my idea of heaven.

As it happened, the bursary that allowed me to go to university helped me begin another adventure and opened up opportunities of a future for me in ways I never could have fathomed.

Ellen: My Inner Compass

In 1952, I was not yet eighteen years old, David was twenty, and we loved each other very much. All the girls at the B'nai Brith youth group envied my good fortune to have this special young man as my boyfriend. Not only was David handsome, with his dark brown hair, blue eyes and six-foot-three height, he was also well spoken, smart and already the owner of his own printing shop. His parents had an older and a younger daughter, and David was their only son. When David took me to meet his family, Mr. and Mrs. Foster were very welcoming.

Unfortunately, Mrs. Foster suffered from a heart condition caused by rheumatic fever in childhood, and the doctor said that she would fare much better if she was not exposed to the cold of Canadian winters. The Foster family had cousins in California, and they were preparing to move to Los Angeles once their immigration papers were approved. All the Fosters were ready to go except David, who said he would stay in Canada because he would not leave without me. David's parents talked it over with him and found a solution.

One day, David took me to see his printing shop. Mr. Foster, who was also a printer and worked with his son, greeted me. Then, to my total bewilderment, he got down on his knees in front of me and said, "Ellen, we all love you. Will you marry my farshtunkene [rotten] son?" I had heard of a man asking a woman to marry him this way, but I never knew that the man's father would do that. I looked at David in puzzlement; he winked at me and nodded, and so I said, "Yes, I will."

After I became David's fiancée, everything happened quickly. Because I was not yet a Canadian citizen, I had to be married to David to go on the family's immigration application. I said goodbye to the optometrist I worked for and prepared for my wedding. Mrs. Foster's friends made a bridal shower for me and I got lots of useful presents. For a wedding dress I bought a simple pink suit that could be worn on the airplane as well. The small wedding took place in the home of a rabbi on the last day of October. David's parents and sisters were there, and representing my family were my uncle Latzi and his wife, and my sister, Kitty. David and I invited my last set of foster parents and some of our closest friends from B'nai Brith. We had a room booked at the King Edward Hotel for three nights for our honeymoon, and our friends showed up there to celebrate with us in funny costumes because it was Halloween. After this short honeymoon, David and I lived upstairs in his home for about two months, until it was time for Mrs. Foster, Dave's younger sister, Deanna, and me to fly to California, while David and his dad stayed behind until the printing shop was sold; then they would drive to Los Angeles to join us.

I did not hesitate to leave my home at my uncle's or to part with my sister, although I loved them both, because I loved David even more. Just as before, I left a place of security for the sake of love, to live in a faraway country among people who did not really know me, trusting that I would be safe and that my and David's love would last forever.

Along with my few belongings, I took with me my inner compass, which even now continues to guide me. Unlike photographs, which keep a record of our physical development as it unfolds through the different stages of our lives and are to be seen by everyone, our inner world is something else. Because of my trusting nature, I learned to protect my inner world from others who would harm it with their criticism and scorn. Feelings are very fragile and can easily be hurt by the belittling judgments of others. My compass told me that one need not be so open, that one must hold back from fully disclosing one's fantasies, pain, joy, lust, sexual pleasures, love, hate, fear and humility, and especially one's anger. My compass reminded me how to protect my talents and my morality from destruction. It told me to keep my opinions and feelings about religion and politics to myself, and to disclose them only when I was sure the goodwill of another person was genuine. It said that human beings are complex and what is on the surface is not always what is inside, and that it takes time to really get to know an individual, and if we are lucky, we can trust a few. I came to the conclusion that in spite of this, trust is the key to open this inner world of ours to help connect us to others on this earth and to make our existence worthwhile.

I want to pass this compass on to my children and grandchild and to those who wish to include themselves among those trusted others, so that it can help them avoid the many hurts that careless and selfish people might direct at them and that might divert them from their destination of serenity and self-respect as they sail through the rough sea of life. As you look for a companion to share the travels of your life, look for the one who can share in harmony. Beware of what can happen when the two lives that join together do not match; when they, like oil and water, do not blend; or like thunder and lightning, they create heat, fear and friction. There is a danger in not wanting to overlook a partner's real or imagined shortcomings.

The compass of my life says this: first of all, we do have choices; second, to be aware of them, we have to become observant of what is really going on around us and pay attention to the circumstances in relationships. Build up your inner strength, from which you can draw to withstand pressures from others when they lean heavily on you. Do not fool yourself that things will change, because just as a leopard cannot change its spots, neither can people who like to hurt or exploit others stop themselves from doing so. If you always get the short end of the stick, if the relationship is unbalanced and one-sided, gather all your strength, leave and look elsewhere for fulfillment. Life is too short to be so easily sacrificed to one who seeks to bind you.

My compass now, just as it has all through the travels of my life, tells me to continually seek my independence, not only to fight for my survival and the reclaiming of my life, but also to build more strength through an ongoing mastering of knowledge. It tells me it is good to be independent, and that I have as much right to be here as anyone else.

Kitty: Destiny Fulfilled

University College was only one streetcar ride away from our house, but it was so different from the neighbourhood I had been living in for four years, it seemed as if it was part of another universe. This secular college was one of several undergraduate colleges that were part of the University of Toronto, and the students there were a mix of religious and ethnic backgrounds. This was in contrast with the other colleges at the university, which were affiliated with traditional religious institutions of Canada, and this was quite likely the reason my guidance counsellor chose it. I had no idea that there was any religious difference between the students attending classes in this building and those in some of the other buildings on the university's grounds. In my mind, people chose different colleges only because they wanted to study specialized subjects taught at a university level in particular professions. Many of the students at University College were Jewish and some, like me, had come from another country. On the corner of College and St. George streets was a large research library, open to the public, and from College to Bloor were a variety of fraternity houses, a large residential building for students who came from out of town and Hillel House, which was a kind of community centre for Jewish students, who could go there for a break or to socialize between their classes.

In the first year of the undergraduate program, students had to take six subjects but did not have to choose a major. I signed up for English, which was required, and geography because it related to science and we had to have a science course. I continued my French studies because I still hoped that one day I would get a second chance to go to Paris – but this time with the ability to communicate. I took Canadian history because it was a subject taught in the Grade 10 class that I had skipped, and as a future teacher, I thought I should know some of the history of the country I lived in. The art and archeology course not only had lectures but a studio program as well, so I very much wanted to be part of it. I also signed up for psychology because it fit into to my timetable.

In spite of my inclination to be studious, my main focus that year was not academic but social. Without any guarantee of more than the one year at university because of my lack of money and my foster parents' opposition to a higher education for women, I thought that this might be my only chance to experience learning of all sorts at this level. So I joined the International Students' Club, became one of the reporters for the *Varsity*, a newspaper run by the students, and for good measure I was cast as Aunt Trina in a play called *I Remember Mama*, which was eventually performed in the Museum Theatre. With all these extracurricular activities, I now wonder how I ever found time for my studies as well, but I did.

I was still smarting from Harvey's rejection, and now that September had come and gone, I stopped waiting for him. Having an hour's between my classes, I stopped in at Hillel House. There in the common room sat a most good-looking young man – looking quite bored. Never being shy, I introduced myself and asked him what he was doing. He said his name was Dov Chetner and he had recently returned from Israel, where he had been part of the volunteer army; now that the state was established, he was continuing his studies. I was quite impressed, since I knew how much courage it took for people to defend Israel as the homeland of the Jews, even though five years earlier, I had not wanted to fight. Reluctantly, I had to leave him because I was already late for my class. Instead of just saying goodbye, I said, "I hope to see you around," and he said that he hoped so, too.

The weekend went by, and that Monday I had a spare after my English class. University College had a beautiful library with long oak tables in the centre of a large study hall. As soon as I entered this room of knowledge, my eyes focused on the young man sitting at some distance, intently studying something. Without hesitation I sat down beside him and said, "Hello, Dov, it is so nice to see you again."

Looking up, he seemed a bit surprised, so I reminded him that we had met a few days earlier at Hillel House. He then asked, "What was your name again?" So I told him again: "It is Kitty Moses," and then I asked him what he was working on. Dov answered that he was supposed to be teaching geometry to a group of young students the next day as part of his assignment as a student teacher. He said that he was not too sure how to go about proving a theorem because he had never taken geometry. I was delighted to show him the steps of a proof, since I had recently studied geometry as part of my Grade 13 program. After about thirty minutes I cleared up his confusion, and he seemed much relieved. He thanked me and invited me to watch him referee the football game that was to take place in the next half-hour on the sports field behind University College.

During high school, I had never attended any of the games that were so popular with my peers. I was never good at sports, nor did I take any interest in the various aspects of physical education. Consequently, I knew nothing about organized sport of any kind. But this time I jumped at the chance to learn more about sports just to get another chance to see him. I promised that I would be there, and I kept my promise. That was the first time I ever watched a football game. I was so ignorant that I had to ask another student to point out which of the players was the referee.

A few days went by. I buckled down to my studies as assignments began to pile up in all my subjects, but I kept hoping to meet Dov again. I was taken with this young man because he was not only a volunteer soldier for Israel but also a future teacher and an athlete. Besides, he was a real grown-up man, not just a high school student like Harvey.

As luck would have it, I bumped into him again at the research library. I went right up to him and said, "Hi, Dov. It is good to see you again. I was wondering how the geometry lesson turned out. Were you able to show your students how to prove the theorem?" He looked at me and said, "Kitty, I don't teach." That was a weird thing for him to say, I thought, after I had spent so much time showing him how to prove the theorem. But I did not give up, and continued the conversation: "You know – after the library I went to see you referee the football game." He looked at me again, possibly thinking I was out of my mind, and said, "Kitty, I don't referee football." It finally dawned on me that the other young man I had met was not Dov. I felt totally stupid and embarrassed. I slunk away, wondering who on earth the young man was, how he could look so much like Dov, why he hadn't said he did not know me, and what he thought of me.

After this fiasco I decided I had better stop chasing boys and start concentrating on my studies, which I loved. I also had to find a way to modify my heavy Hungarian accent if I ever wanted to work as a teacher. My French instructor, Professor Joliat, was an excellent teacher and I was a good student in French. I went to him and explained my problem. I told him that I only had money for this school year, and in order for me to become an elementary school teacher I needed to speak more like a Canadian. I was wondering if I could learn to speak English properly in the French phonics lab because there was no equipment elsewhere to learn proper pronunciation of English. That fine gentleman not only agreed to let me use the French language laboratory, he even got his Canadian wife to teach me, using the equipment, to enunciate the variety of sounds correctly and to approximate standard Canadian speech patterns. I never eradicated my accent, but I pronounced English well enough that by springtime, after my second interview, I was accepted to Teachers' College unconditionally.

~

October was almost over when one of my new friends at school said to me, "Kitty, there's this guy, Irving Salsberg, who keeps going all around campus and Hillel House, trying to find you or get your phone number." Of course he had trouble finding my phone number, because although I had told him my full name, I lived with my foster parents. I felt flattered that he was searching for me, almost as if I were Cinderella, so when he finally phoned and asked me for a date, I said yes without any hesitation. He told me that we would be driving to Haliburton, north of Toronto, because he needed to check up on the camp he had been in charge of in the summer.

He called for me that Saturday morning, dressed in faded blue jeans, a lumberjack shirt and a leather Argos jacket. When Daddy Feingold opened the door to let him in, neither of us was impressed by his Argos jacket; both of us were too ignorant about sports to realize that owning one was a status symbol. Daddy was bothered that Irving had obviously not shaved for a couple of days. Still, I went on the outing, and on the way we talked, learning about each other. I do not remember just what we said, but I know I was impressed that this young man had been given the responsibility for Camp Northland as acting director. At the age of twenty-three, he was in charge of more than four hundred campers and staff. On this autumn trip, he had to make sure that all the buildings and cabins were properly secured for winter, and that if there remained anything to repair it would get done before the campers and staff arrived the following summer. Again I was impressed.

But just as I did not understand the status implied by the Argos jacket, I also did not truly understand the extent of a camp director's responsibility when he is in charge of so many youngsters away from home. Perhaps my ignorance was a help to me. Irving was a popular guy, both because he was an athlete and because of his position at camp. I am sure I did not show the same enthusiasm in having him for a date that he was probably used to being shown by other girls. Instead, I felt very flattered that he had gone to all that trouble in finding me and when, on our return to the city, he asked me to go to the movies with him the following day, I happily accepted. This time when Irving arrived, he was clean shaven and was wearing well-pressed grey flannel trousers, a freshly ironed shirt and a dark blue blazer with a large university crest on it. Daddy was duly impressed. He called me over to the kitchen and whispered, "Kitty, you should always go out with nice boys like this, not the bum you went out with yesterday." From that day on, I don't think I gave Harvey any more thought.

Irving had already finished his degree in physical and health education and was completing his teaching certificate at the Faculty of Education. Coming from a poor immigrant family, he worked full-time during the summers and part-time during the winters to put himself through school. We saw each other steadily, but not often, because we both were committed to doing well at school. I fell in love not only with Irving but with being at university as well, and I didn't want to leave for teachers' college. I was obliged to go the following September, but I found out that the university had programs for part-time students and I could attend during summer and part-time during winter also. This seemed a perfect way for me to continue my studies, get a teaching certificate *and* earn a living.

On New Year's Eve, a month after my twentieth birthday, Irving asked me to marry him. He said that with both of us working as teachers we would be able to buy a small house. I did not care if we had to live in a tent. By now, not only I but my foster parents as well were in love with him, and Daddy Feingold told me that my mother must have talked with God on my behalf to have such a wonderful boy sent to me for a husband.

I went to teachers' college the following September, carried on corresponding with my sister, who by now was living in California, and in the evenings I continued my university education. By the end of the school year, I was practise-teaching in Toronto. I had the most unusual good luck: I was sent to a school where the teacher in charge was Mrs. Brooks, the former Grade 11 teacher at Bloor Collegiate who marked the Grade 11 exam paper I took by mistake. She was delighted to see me after four years, and wrote a glowing report about the quality of my teaching and the excellent rapport I had with the students in her class. With such a report, I didn't have much trouble getting my first teaching job in Toronto. By this time, Irving had been teaching for a year in Forest Hill. He bought a small house for us, and we got married on August 29, 1954, the anniversary of my arrival in Canada on the *Aquitania* six years earlier. On the simple golden wedding ring that Irving gave me, which I will wear forever, he had the jeweller inscribe: "For the Library, Love Irving."

I am sure that I was not the most traditional "little wife" for those times. In the first place, Irving had to teach me how to cook because Mom Feingold never did, and I can't say that I would have been an eager student if she had. As well, he was not quite prepared for, but accepted very graciously, my wanting a family that would include not only our own children but quite a few foster children as well. He was proud of my achievements and overlooked my many faults. I, on the other hand, could not even find any faults in him and admired him without reservation. I wish my parents could have seen the beauty of their daughter's life with her family. Some people say they have – and still do.

Glossary

American Jewish Joint Distribution Committee (JDC) Also known colloquially as the "Joint." A charitable organization founded in 1914 to provide humanitarian assistance and relief to Jews all over the world in times of crisis. The Joint provided material support for persecuted Jews in Germany and other Nazi-occupied territories and facilitated their immigration to neutral countries such as Portugal, Turkey and China. Between 1939 and 1944, JDC officials helped close to 81,000 European Jews find asylum in various parts of the world. Between 1944 and 1947, the JDC assisted more than 100,000 refugees living in DP camps by offering retraining programs, cultural activities and financial assistance for emigration.

Allies The coalition of countries that fought against Germany, Italy and Japan (the Axis nations). At the beginning of World War II in September 1939, the coalition included France, Poland and Britain. Once Germany invaded the USSR in June 1941 and the United States entered the war following the bombing of Pearl Harbor by Japan on December 7, 1941, the main leaders of the Allied powers became Britain, the USSR and the United States. Other Allies included Canada, Australia, Czechoslovakia, Greece, Mexico, Brazil, South Africa and China.

antisemitism Prejudice, discrimination, persecution and/or hatred against Jewish people, institutions, culture and symbols.

Arrow Cross Party (in Hungarian, Nyilaskeresztes Párt – Hungarista Mozgalom; abbreviation: Nyilas) A Hungarian nationalistic and antisemitic party founded by Ferenc Szálasi in 1935 under the name the Party of National Will. With the full support of Nazi Germany, the newly renamed Arrow Cross Party ran in Hungary's 1939 election and won 25 per cent of the vote. The party was banned shortly after the elections, but was legalized again in March 1944 when Germany occupied Hungary. Under Nazi approval, the party assumed control of Hungary from October 15, 1944, to March 1945, led by Szálasi under the name the Government of National Unity. The Arrow Cross regime was particularly brutal toward Jews – in addition to the thousands of Hungarian Jews who had been deported to Nazi death camps during the previous Miklós Horthy regime, the Arrow Cross, during their short period of rule, instigated the murder of tens of thousands of Hungarian Jews. In one specific incident on November 8, 1944, more than 70,000 Jews were rounded up and sent on a death march to Nazi camps in Austria. Between December 1944 and January 1945, the Arrow Cross murdered approximately 20,000 Jews, many of whom had been forced into a closed ghetto at the end of November 1944. *See also* Danube River.

assimilation A term used to refer to the cultural assimilation and social integration of Jews into the surrounding culture. Before the eighteenth century many European countries, including Hungary and Czechoslovakia, restricted where Jewish people could live and excluded them from certain professions, educational opportunities and land ownership. In 1849 new laws in the Austrian Empire permitted free movement for Jews of Bohemia and Moravia, and in 1867 the Jews of Hungary were granted full equality. For many Jews this emancipation resulted in a modernization of Jewish religious and cultural practices, including language, clothing, customs, professions and cultural life.

Auschwitz (German; in Polish, Oświęcim) A town in southern Poland approximately forty kilometres from Krakow, it is also the name of the largest complex of Nazi concentration camps that were built nearby. The Auschwitz complex contained three main camps: Auschwitz I, a slave labour camp built in May 1940; Auschwitz II-Birkenau, a death camp built in early 1942; and Auschwitz-Monowitz, a slave labour camp built in October 1942. In 1941, Auschwitz I was a testing site for usage of the lethal gas Zyklon B as a method of mass killing, which then went into wide usage. Between 1942 and 1944, transports arrived at Auschwitz-Birkenau from almost every country in Europe; approximately 435,000 Hungarian Jews were deported to Auschwitz between May 15 and July 8, 1944. It is estimated that 1.1 million people were murdered in Auschwitz; approximately 950,000 were Jewish; 74,000 Polish; 21,000 Roma; 15,000 Soviet prisoners of war; and 10,000–15,000 other nationalities. The Auschwitz complex was liberated by the Soviet army in January 1945.

bar mitzvah, bat mitzvah (Hebrew; literally, son/daughter of the commandment) The time when, in Jewish tradition, children become religiously and morally responsible for their actions and are considered adults for the purpose of synagogue and other rituals. Traditionally this occurs at age thirteen for boys and twelve for girls. Historically, girls were not included in this ritual until the latter half of the twentieth century, when liberal Jews instituted an equivalent ceremony and celebration for girls called a bat mitzvah. A bar/bat mitzvah marks the attainment of adulthood by a ceremony during which the boy/girl is called upon to read a portion of the Torah and recite the prescribed prayers in a public prayer service.

B'nai Brith (Hebrew; Children of the Covenant) A volunteer-based Jewish communal agency founded in New York in 1843. Through its branches in more than fifty countries, it provides services for seniors, combats antisemitism and advocates for human rights.

Budapest ghetto The area established by the government of Hungary on November 29, 1944. By December 10, the ghetto and its 33,000 Jewish inhabitants were sealed off from the rest of the city. At the end of December, Jews who had previously held "protected" status (many through the Swedish government) were moved into the ghetto and the number of residents increased to 55,000; by January 1945, the number had reached 70,000. The ghetto was overcrowded and lacked sufficient food, water and sanitation. Supplies dwindled and conditions worsened during the Soviet siege of Budapest and thousands died of starvation and disease. Soviet forces liberated the ghetto on January 18, 1945. *See also* ghetto.

Canadian Jewish Congress (cjc) An advocacy organization and lobbying group for the Canadian Jewish community from 1919 to 2011. In 1947, the cjc convinced the Canadian government to re-issue Privy Council Order 1647 – originally adopted in 1942 to admit five hundred Jewish refugee children from Vichy France, although they never made it out – that allowed for one thousand Jewish children under the age of eighteen to be admitted to Canada. Under the auspices of the cjc, which would provide for the refugees' care, the War Orphans Project was established in April 1947 and the cjc began searching for Jewish war orphans with the help of the United Nations Relief and Rehabilitation Administration (unrra). Between 1947 and 1949, 1,123 young Jewish refugees came to Canada. The cjc was restructured in 2007 and its functions subsumed under the Centre for Israel and Jewish Affairs (cija) in 2011.

catechism A reference text and guide to the Catholic religion, in a question-and-answer format, to help teach the doctrine of the faith.

circumcision Removal of the foreskin of the penis. In Judaism, ritual circumcision is performed on the eighth day of a male infant's life in a religious ceremony known as a *brit milah* (Hebrew) or *bris* (Yiddish) to welcome him into the covenant between God and the People of Israel.

Danube River The second longest river in Europe, running through ten European countries, including Hungary. It is an important source of drinking water and mode of transportation for millions of Europeans. During the winter of 1944–1945, members of the Arrow Cross rounded up Jews from the streets and the nearby Budapest ghetto, marched them to the shore of the Danube and shot them so that their bodies would fall into the river to be carried away. A memorial consisting of sixty pairs of rusted, cast-iron shoes was erected on the site in 2005. *See also* Arrow Cross Party.

Eichmann, Adolf (1906–1962) The head of the Gestapo department responsible for the implementation of the Nazis' policy of mass murder of Jews (the so-called Final Solution), Eichmann was in charge of transporting Jews to death camps in Poland. In 1942, Eichmann coordinated deportations of Jewish populations from Slovakia, the Netherlands, France and Belgium. In 1944, he was directly involved in the deportations of Jews from Hungary, as well as in negotiations to supply Jews for slave labour in Austria. After the war, Eichmann escaped from US custody and fled to Argentina, where he was captured in 1960 by Israeli intelligence operatives; his ensuing 1961 trial in Israel was widely and internationally televised. Eichmann was sentenced to death and hanged in May 1962. *See also* Final Solution.

Final Solution (in German, *Die Endlösung der Judenfrage*) Euphemistic term referring to the "Final Solution to the Jewish Question," the Nazi plan for the systematic murder of Europe's Jewish population between 1941 and 1945.

Folks Shule (Yiddish; literally, people's school) A secular public school established in various cities in Canada in the early twentieth century.

Flossenbürg The fourth concentration camp built in Germany, established in 1938. About 100 subcamps were established around Flossenbürg to provide labour for German arms production. By March 1945, about 53,000 prisoners were being held in the Flossenbürg camp system; about 14,500 were in the main camp. Three days before liberation, 14,000 prisoners were forced from Flossenbürg on a death march. On April 26, 1945, the survivors of the death march were retrieved by a US army unit.

ghetto A confined residential area for Jews. The term originated in Venice, Italy, in 1516 with a law requiring all Jews to live on a segregated, gated island known as Ghetto Nuovo. Throughout the Middle Ages in Europe, Jews were often forcibly confined to gated Jewish neighbourhoods. During the Holocaust, the Nazis forced Jews to live in crowded and unsanitary conditions in rundown districts of cities and towns. *See also* Budapest ghetto.

gimnázium (Hungarian; in German, *Gymnasium*) A word used throughout Central and Eastern Europe to mean high school or secondary school.

hora An Israeli folk dance that is performed by a group in a circle and is traditionally danced on celebratory occasions.

Jewish houses (Budapest) Also known as "yellow star" buildings (*sárga csillagos házak*). In June 1944, three months after Germany occupied Hungary, the Nazis ordered the Jews in Budapest to move into designated buildings marked with a yellow Star of David. More than 200,000 Jews were assigned to fewer than two thousand apartments. They were allowed to leave the buildings for two hours in the afternoon, but only if they wore an identifying yellow Star of David on their clothing. This meant they could be easily located when the time came for them to be deported. *See also* ghetto; yellow star.

Jewish laws (Hungary) A series of four laws passed in Hungary between May 1938 and the spring of 1942 that restricted Jewish participation in the broader society. The laws limited Jewish membership in professional organizations; defined Jewishness on a racial basis and excluded foreign-born Jews from Hungarian citizenship; banned mixed marriages and banned Jews from owning property; introduced forced labour; and legalized the forced relocation of Jews. *See also* Labour Service.

kapo (German) A concentration camp prisoner appointed by the SS to oversee other prisoners as slave labourers.

kashrut A system of rules in Jewish tradition that regulates what can be eaten, how food is prepared and served, and how animals and poultry are slaughtered for meat. Foods that are prepared according to these rules are considered to be kosher.

Labour Service (in Hungarian, *Munkaszolgálat*) Hungary's military-related labour service system, which was first established in 1919 for those considered too "politically unreliable" for regular military service. After the labour service was made compulsory in 1939, Jewish men of military age were recruited to serve; however, having been deemed "unfit" to bear arms, they were equipped with tools and employed in mining, road and rail construction and maintenance work. Though the men were treated relatively well at first, the system became increasingly punitive in nature. By 1941, Jews in forced labour battalions were required to wear a yellow armband and civilian clothes; they had no formal rank and were unarmed; they were often mistreated by extremely anti-semitic supervisors; and their work included clearing minefields, causing their death. Between 20,000 and 40,000 Jewish men died during their forced labour service.

Mauthausen A notoriously brutal Nazi concentration camp located about twenty kilometres east of the Austrian city of Linz. First established in 1938 shortly after the annexation of Austria to imprison "asocial" political opponents of the Third Reich, the camp grew to encompass fifty nearby subcamps and became the largest forced labour complex in the German-occupied territories. By the end of the war, close to 200,000 prisoners had passed through the Mauthausen forced labour camp system and almost 120,000 of them died there – including 38,120 Jews – from starvation, disease and hard labour. The US army liberated the camp on May 5, 1945.

Miha orphanages (Yiddish; abbreviation for *mittel-hachsharah*, middle training) A network of children's homes, or orphanages, established in 1935 and run by American and international Jewish communal organizations. After World War II, these organizations took responsibility for finding and, if necessary, ransoming Jewish children placed with Christian families so that the children could be reunited with surviving family members or returned to Jewish communities. The orphanages offered programs that combined academic instruction and vocational training; some also prepared children for immigration to pre-state Israel.

polgári (Hungarian; literally, civil) A term referring to publicly funded junior high schools for ten- to fourteen-year-old children.

Sachsenhausen (also known as Oranienburg) A concentration camp located north of Berlin, Germany. It was established to imprison political prisoners and "subversive elements."

treif (Yiddish; also treyf) Food that is not allowed under Jewish dietary laws. *See also* kashrut.

yellow star (also known as a Star of David; in Hebrew, *Magen David*) The six-pointed star that is the ancient and most recognizable symbol of Judaism. During World War II, Jews in Nazi-occupied areas were frequently forced to wear a badge or armband with the Star of David on it as an identifying mark of their lesser status and to single them out as targets for persecution.

Zionism A movement promoted by the Viennese Jewish journalist Theodor Herzl, who argued in his 1896 book *Der Judenstaat* (The Jewish State) that the best way to resolve the problem of antisemitism and persecution of Jews in Europe was to create an independent Jewish state in the historic Jewish homeland of Biblical Israel. Zionists also promoted the revival of Hebrew as a Jewish national language.

Photographs

1

2

1   The family of Kitty and Ellen's mother, Borishka Federer, in Budapest, Hungary,
    circa 1914. From left to right: Kitty and Ellen's aunt Gizi; their mother, Borishka;
    their uncle, Latzi; their grandmother, Franceska; and their aunt Margaret.
2   Federer family, circa 1916. From left to right: Kitty and Ellen's grandfather, Ignace
    Federer; Latzi; Borishka; Gizi; Franceska; and Margaret.

Marton Mozes Nagy, Kitty and Ellen's father, circa 1930.

Kitty, age two, with her mother and her paternal grandmother, Mutter. Budapest, circa 1933.

Four-year-old Ellen (left) and six-year-old Kitty (right), soon after Ellen's recovery from dysentery. Budapest, 1939.

Kitty, age ten, circa 1942.

Ellen, age eight, 1944. A fragment of the mandatory yellow star can be seen in the lower left corner of the photograph.

1   Kitty and Ellen's cousins, Hedi and Imre, after the war. Budapest, circa 1948.
2   Aunt Margaret (far left) with her business partner Mrs. Benedikt and Uncle Vili
     at their stall in the Lehel Market. Budapest, 1946.

Kitty, age seventeen, in front of Casa Loma. 1949.

1

2

1 Ellen, age fourteen, practising her dancing. 1949.
2 Ellen, circa 1950s, Toronto.

Kitty and Irving Salsberg (centre) celebrating their wedding with Kitty's foster parents, Chaika and Shloime Feingold. August 29, 1954.

1 Kitty's family in Toronto. Back row, left to right: Kitty's son, Martin Thomas; Irving's father, Moisha Salsberg; Kitty's daughter Sharon; and Kitty's foster mother, Chaika Feingold. Front row, left to right: Kitty's daughter Barbara; Kitty's husband, Irving Salsberg; Kitty's daughter Mindy, and Kitty. Circa 1965.

2 Kitty with her immediate family. From left to right: Mindy, Kitty, Martin Thomas, Irving and Sharon. In front: Barbara. Circa 1970.

Ellen with her husband and in-laws in Los Angeles, 1955. From left to right: Ellen's husband, David; Ellen; her mother-in-law, Josephine; her father-in-law, Burt; and her sister-in-law, Deanna.

1

2

1   Ellen in Los Angeles with her children. Left to right: Barry, Rachel, Martin and Stephen. Circa 1964.

2   Ellen's family in Los Angeles. From left to right: Ellen's son Stephen; Ellen; her son Martin; Martin's wife, Kathleen; and Ellen's husband, David Foster.

1

2

1 Kitty and Ellen reuniting with their cousins Hedi and Imre in Budapest, 1983.
From left to right: Imre, Kitty, Hedi and Ellen.

2 Ellen visiting family in Toronto. From left to right: Ellen, Auntie Helen Schlesinger, Kitty's son, Martin Thomas, and Kitty.

Kitty and Ellen, 1991.

Index

The Azrieli Foundation was established in 1989 to realize and extend the philanthropic vision of David J. Azrieli, C.M., C.Q., M.Arch. The Foundation's mission is to support a wide spectrum of initiatives in education and research. The Azrieli Foundation is an active supporter of programs in the fields of Education, the education of architects, scientific and medical research, and the arts. The Azrieli Foundation's many initiatives include: the Holocaust Survivor Memoirs Program, which collects, preserves, publishes and distributes the written memoirs of survivors in Canada; the Azrieli Institute for Educational Empowerment, an innovative program successfully working to keep at-risk youth in school; the Azrieli Fellows Program, which promotes academic excellence and leadership on the graduate level at Israeli universities; the Azrieli Music Project, which celebrates and fosters the creation of high-quality new Jewish orchestral music; and the Azrieli Neurodevelopmental Research Program, which supports advanced research on neurodevelopmental disorders, particularly Fragile X and Autism Spectrum Disorders.